CREATE A CARD
with stickers, stencils, and stamps

CREATE A CARD
with stickers, stencils, and stamps

STEPHANIE WEIGHTMAN

NEW HOLLAND

First published in 2005 by
New Holland Publishers (UK) Ltd
London • Cape Town • Sydney • Auckland

Garfield House
86–88 Edgware Road
London W2 2EA

80 McKenzie Street
Cape Town 8001
South Africa

Level 1, Unit 4
14 Aquatic Drive
Frenchs Forest, NSW 2086
Australia

218 Lake Road
Northcote
Auckland
New Zealand

ISBN 1 84537 052 X

Senior Editor: Corinne Masciocchi
Designer: Peter Crump
Photographer: Shona Wood
Editorial Director: Rosemary Wilkinson
Production: Hazel Kirkman

Printed in the USA

This book I dedicate to my sister Zoë, my
business partner and best friend.

Acknowledgments

Firstly, I'd like to thank you, the reader—
beginners and experienced card makers
alike—because without you and the
extraordinary passion that card makers
exude, books like this would only ever be
a dream.

There are so many people I need to
thank: the team at New Holland; special
thanks go to Corinne and Clare for their
unfailing patience, to Shona for her
unrivaled talent, and to Rosemary for
giving me the opportunity to write
another book. I also have to say a huge
thank you to my team at work, especially
Debbie and Zoë, whom even through late
nights and a busy year pulled out all the
stops to help. If anyone has been missed
off I can only say please forgive me for
being so absorbed in such an exciting
book. Thank you everyone.

contents

Introduction

Some of my first childhood memories are of gluing and sticking down pieces of paper. As an adult, making cards allows me to indulge this memory and put it to good use. Like all crafts, card making is a therapeutic but nevertheless addictive hobby. If it is something you have never done I urge you to have a try. It is so simple to make professional-looking cards that, together with a few simple instructions and top tips, you will be amazed at just how easy and rewarding it is.

Creating handmade cards has in recent years become very fashionable, so much so that you will find many card and gift stores selling "hand-finished" greeting cards. How many times have you walked out of a card store thinking "I could make that card?" I hope this book inspires you to do just that. Using a multitude of products and techniques, there are over 35 card-making projects for both beginners and the more advanced crafters.

The book is divided into three main chapters that include the techniques and a selection of beautiful projects for stickers, stencils, and stamps.

Stickers are a great starting point: they are simple to use, yet create stunning effects. They are often bought readymade or designed to simply sit on the front of a card, but you can also make your own stickers at home. There are almost no limits to what you can design or achieve!

Stencils were traditionally made from mylar plastic or oiled manila card and were—and still are—used with stencil creams, stencil paints, or decorative chalks applied to the stencil and onto the chosen support. Stencils now come in flexible plastic with a self-adhesive surface that bonds tightly to the support, allowing you to use any number of coloring implements without any bleeding. These are very versatile because they are washable and therefore reusable. Stencils also come in a large number of metals to create raised paper impressions such as those done with dry embossing or to use as templates to cut design patterns.

Stamping is a card-making craft that has been around for a number of years, but if you have never tried it before you will find simple projects to get you started, and if you are an experienced stamper you will find new ideas and inspiration.

There is something for everyone so I hope you enjoy making the various card projects in this book as much as sending them to your loved ones.

Stephanie Weightman

Tools and materials

Making greeting cards can be as quick and easy or as intricate as you choose to make it. You can start with a simple set of tools and materials such as a pair of good-quality scissors and a selection of interesting colored papers. As you become more involved, you may like to invest in a large carry case or box to store all your craft products so that they are close to hand. Below is a selection of tools and materials that are useful for card making.

Cards and glues, rulers and scissors

1 card stock there is a wide range of different cards and papers on the market. Commercially made papers come in sizes ranging from 33$\frac{1}{8}$ x 23$\frac{1}{3}$ in (84 x 59 cm) to 11$\frac{3}{4}$ x 8$\frac{1}{4}$ in (30 x 21 cm). Most of the cards in this book use a weight of approximately 172 to 203 lbs (280 to 330 gsm or grams per square meter) for the main card stock.

2 glue stick multi-purpose glue used mainly for layering backing cards.

3 adhesive paste used to stick down 3-D embellishments or as a sticky layer to sprinkle with glitter.

4 glue dots come in a selection of sizes. Simply take the card or embellishment to the glue dot, remove the dot from the backing sheet, and position in place.

5 3-D foam glue pads used for 3-D decoupage and to raise card and paper from the surface they are mounted on. The pads are usually about $\frac{1}{4}$-in (0.4-cm) thick with adhesive on both sides.

6 mini glue dots usually come on a 5$\frac{3}{4}$ x 4$\frac{1}{8}$-in (15 x 11-cm) sheet. Simply press the surface you want to stick down to the glue dots and peel back: the dots will stick to the surface. Ideal for use on vellum because these small dots are almost invisible.

7 spray adhesive available in repositionable or permanent varieties. The former is useful when you are planning a card and are not ready to secure everything permanently in place. Sprays are usually solvent-based so you will need to work in a well-ventilated area.

8 low tack masking tape always a handy craft material to have in your box. Great for holding down stencils and especially useful when securing a design before cutting with a craft knife.

9 metal ruler invest in a metal ruler for cutting and scoring cards.

10 plastic ruler a clear plastic ruler is good for lining up and measuring at the same time.

11 decorative edge scissors great for creating border effects. Draw a line with a pencil and ruler and use it as a guide when cutting with the scissors.

Decorative papers and stickers

1 outline stickers commonly referred to as peel-offs, they are inexpensive and available in a number of designs. They are easy to use and make quick and colorful cards.

2 mulberry paper semiopaque handmade paper made from mulberry leaves and silk strands. It can be expensive so use in small quantities.

3 talcum powder applied to the back of premade stickers to prevent unwanted areas of glue from sticking to card stock.

4 vellum sheer paper with a subtle translucent finish, available in a wide range of colors.

5 printed vellum sheer paper printed with a wide range of designs and colors. Look out for coordinating plain and patterned paper ranges.

6 metallic and holographic decorative cards these cards give a striking look to handmade cards. Available in a good range of colors and a variety of eye-catching patterns.

7 rubdown stickers rub over the sticker with a Popsicle stick through the protective film onto your chosen surface. Suitable for use on paper and wooden and glass surfaces.

8 holographic outline stickers second generation of outline stickers or peels-offs designed to create simple but effective greeting cards.

9 micro bead stickers premade stickers coated with micro beads to create a textured finish.

10 prefinished stickers designed to make card making simple; just peel and stick.

Pens, pencils, and paints

1 stencil paints a good painting medium to add color to your cards. Watercolor paints are also subtle so use them when you want to achieve a more delicate finish.

2 glitter glue comes in different colors and applicator sizes to control the flow of the glue.

3 fiber tip pens available in a huge array of colors and inexpensive to buy.

4 gel pens come in a rainbow of colors to include sparkles and metallic. The ink is opaque and works beautifully on dark-colored cards.

5 brush markers double-ended fiber tip pens with a narrow point for intricate work and a wider one for covering larger areas.

6 coloring pencils and watercolor pencils choose the best quality you can afford. Colors can be blended together to create other shades.

7 kneadable eraser a good-quality eraser is essential if you want to remove pencil lines completely. Kneadable erasers are very versatile because they can be molded to a point.

8 pencil use an HB pencil for guidelines to cut and a 2B pencil or softer for lines you know you will want to rub out.

9 pencil sharpener safer to use than a craft knife for sharpening pencils.

10 round paintbrush good for general painting. A good-quality brush will have a smooth tip for detail work. Synthetic brushes are ideal for card coloring.

11 angle paintbrush good for double-loading paint (putting two colors on a brush at a time), to allow you to color shade and highlight at the same time.

12 decorating chalks available in a large range of colors and designed to give a soft finish. Apply with cotton buds or stencil brushes. To avoid smudging, fix with a spray of fixative.

Card-making tools and materials

1 light box used for tracing designs and for dry stencil embossing.

2 embossing stencil metal stencil used in conjunction with a light box and an embossing tool for a technique referred to as dry embossing.

3 cutting mat always choose a self-healing cutting mat because the surface will close back over the cuts you have made and will remain smooth. Never use the cutting mat when embossing with a heat tool because this will cause the mat to buckle.

4 guillotine it is now possible to buy small lightweight guillotines that are very useful for cutting paper and card and are easier to use than rolling blade cutters.

5 sticker maker converts small embellishments into stickers by applying an even surface of glue to the reverse of the embellishment.

6 ribbler this handheld machine simply and quickly corrugates card as it is fed through the rollers. If you like working with corrugated card then invest in one of these: it will soon cover the cost of purchasing finished corrugated card.

7 craft knife a good-quality sharp craft knife is a must. An interchangeable blade is far better than a snap-off blade. If your budget allows, invest in a swivel blade for cutting curves.

8 scissors you will need a good pair of decoupage scissors especially when you are cutting out intricate designs. Invest in both a small pair and a larger one for use on larger designs.

9 hammer a small hammer that is not too heavy to hold is ideal for using with an eyelet setter. A pin hammer or tacking hammer are both suitable.

10 eyelet mat designed to provided a clean, hard-wearing surface to create eyelet holes without damaging your cutting mat or work surface.

11 hole punch and setter a combination set designed to punch holes into card stock and set the eyelets.

12 eyelets available in a variety of colors and different shapes and sizes.

13 heat gun manufactured for working with paper. Keep your hands off the vents and hold the gun about 6 in (15 cm) from your project to prevent the paper from scorching.

Stencils and stamping

1 wooden stamps made of a wooden block, a piece of mounting foam, and a detail rubber image.

2 metallic stencil cream paints metallic cream color that is great for stenciling. Apply the cream with a stencil brush or cotton bud. Clean the brushes with soap and water after use.

3 stencil brush available in a variety of sizes. Use the appropriate size for the design you are working with.

4 metal stencil template metal templates are extremely durable and mostly used for outlining, cutting, or dry stencil embossing.

5 embossing tool used for scoring paper and card and for stencil embossing.

6 decorative punch available in all shapes and designs, decorative punches are used to repeat a design by punching silhouette paper shapes as decoration.

7 sticky stencil a plastic repositionable, self-adhesive stencil. Wash with warm soapy water and replace onto the carrier sheet after use.

8 embossing stencil a lightweight brass stencil used for dry stencil embossing.

9 pricking tool long, sharp spike on a wooden or plastic handle. A useful tool for making fine, even holes in paper, vellum, or card stock and for lifting off very small stickers.

10 embossing powder sprinkle over wet ink, tap off the excess, and heat with a heat gun to melt the powder and give your design a raised finish.

11 pastel embossing powder soft and subtle color used in the same way as traditional metallic powders. Used to create embossed effects with a heat tool.

12 glitter look for ultra-fine glitter because it is particularly effective for card making.

13 pigment-based ink pad available in clear or tinted, it stays wet for about 10 minutes to allow a longer application time. Used with embossing powder, it creates raised images when rubber stamping.

14 3-D gloss a thick, viscous fluid that is opaque when wet and dries clear. It leaves the surface "glasslike" and raised. Ideal for use on any porous surface.

15 dye-based ink pad water-based and very fast drying, it can be used not only for stamping but also to create watercolor effects using a paintbrush and water.

16 embossing ink pad available in clear or tinted. The ink is slow drying on the card so stays moist while you apply embossing powders to create raised images when stamping.

STICKERS

Fall leaves 16

Daisy, daisy 18

Let's get moving 20

3-D butterflies 30

Christmas bauble 33

Bouquet of flowers 36

Pretty parcel 23

Tulip time 26

Bonny bib 28

Perfect pressed flowers 39

Mini card and envelope 42

Wedding celebration 45

Sticker techniques

Stickers are far more than just an outline or design applied to the front of a card. There are numerous designs to choose from and in this chapter you will find ideas and inspiration on how to make the most of their simplicity. Stickers can be cut out, colored in, and positioned back-to-back to create amazing three-dimensional effects. They are easy to use and so provide the perfect starting point for someone who has never made greeting cards before.

Cutting out to create colored backgrounds

Remove the outline sticker from the backing sheet and stick it onto a piece of colored card. Cut around the edges of the sticker. This card-backed sticker can now be used for embellishing a card. Apply 3-D foam glue pads to the back to add further dimension.

Creating two-tone designs

You will need two different colored outline stickers of the same design. Take the outline of one sticker and stick it onto a piece of white or colored card or acetate. Use the pricking tool to pick up the small background pieces from the other sticker of the same design to fill in the holes of the main sticker.

Coloring in outline stickers with paints

Choose an outline sticker and, using watercolor paints, roughly paint the design of the sticker onto a piece of watercolor paper or good-quality card stock. The paper will have to be quite thick to avoid it cockling. When the paint is dry, stick the sticker over the design and cut out around the edges, ready to use for your card design.

Coloring in outline stickers with permanent markers

To create a stained glass effect, position the outline sticker onto a piece of acetate and use colored permanent marker pens to fill in the background. When dry, cut out leaving a border around the edges of the sticker to allow the acetate to fit in the aperture of a card.

Using rubdown stickers

Rubdowns are a great way to add an embellishment to a card. Choose the rubdown of your choice, cut it out from the backing sheet, and position it onto a piece of card. Using a flat wooden stick, rub over the design applying gentle pressure. Peel off the backing sheet to reveal the rubdown. Layer the card on colored backgrounds to suit the design of your card.

Back-to-back positioning

Stickers can be positioned back to back to create a two-dimensional effect—great for hanging inside aperture cards. Simply select two stickers of the same design and place them back to back. Sandwich thread or fine cord between the two layers and attach inside a card aperture.

Fall leaves

Rich reds, browns, and greens all combine together to make this card stand out from the rest. The unusual shape of the card makes it look more difficult to make than it actually is.

1 Transfer the harmonica template on page 122 onto the burgundy card and mark the fold and cut lines. Working on the cutting mat, cut out the template and cut along the solid lines using a sharp craft knife and a ruler. Fold the card along the central fold and then fold over the top and bottom folds, making sure not to fold the center extension.

2 With the card in the correct position, draw a circle 2½ in (6 cm) in diameter using the pencil and the compass in the middle of the center extension and position the fall leaves around the outline of the circle.

3 Once the circle is complete, position the top embellishment with half the sticker extending past the card's edge. Turn the card over and dab a little talcum powder on the back of the protruding sticker to absorb the glue.

4 Finish off the card by randomly positioning a few fallen leaves to the left-hand side of the card along the bottom edge. ■

Daisy, daisy

Bright, fresh, and funky is the message this card sends out. It is perfect for a young person or someone young at heart and is guaranteed to brighten anyone's day. Makes a great "thinking of you" card.

YOU WILL NEED

11¾ x 8¼-in (30 x 21-cm) yellow card
Guillotine
Ruler
Embossing tool
11¾ x 8¼-in (30 x 21-cm) lime
   green paper

Pencil
Scissors
Glue stick
Three daisy head bead stickers
   in yellow and orange

1 Cut the 11¾ x 8¼-in (30 x 21-cm) yellow card in half lengthwise using the guillotine. Score the card down the center lengthwise, using the ruler and the embossing tool, and fold over.

2 Refer to the leaves and stems templates on page 122 and draw the shapes onto the lime green paper and then cut them out. Crease the leaves in half to create a three-dimensional effect.

3 Position the green stems and leaves on the front of the card and glue them down. Make sure you glue down only one half of each leaf so that the three-dimensional effect is not lost.

4 Carefully remove the daisy head bead stickers one by one from the backing sheet and position them at the top of the stems to complete the card. ■

Let's get moving

Using outline stickers to make this bright and bold card couldn't be easier. It's perfect for friends or family moving into a new home. Using watercolor paints means the colors can be as bold or as subtle as you like.

YOU WILL NEED

Silver house outline sticker
  3¹⁄₂ x 2¹⁄₂ in (8.5 x 6. 5 cm)
Sheet of acetate
Watercolor paints in blue, green, and brown
Water pot

Paintbrush
Paint palette
Two sheets 11³⁄₄ x 8¹⁄₄-in (30 x 21-cm) white
  watercolor card
Ruler

Pencil
Scissors
Sheet of silver border stickers
Glue dots
Embossing tool

1 Carefully remove the house outline sticker from the backing sheet and position it in the center of the piece of acetate.

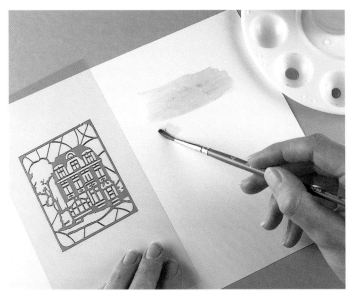

2 Mix a small amount of watercolor paints onto a palette. Use pale blue for the sky, green for the trees and grass, and brown for the house bricks. Using the paintbrush, paint the colors onto one of the 11³⁄₄ x 8¹⁄₄-in (30 x 21-cm) white watercolor cards, placing the outline sticker nearby to use as a guide for the position of the colors. **steps 3–6 ▶**

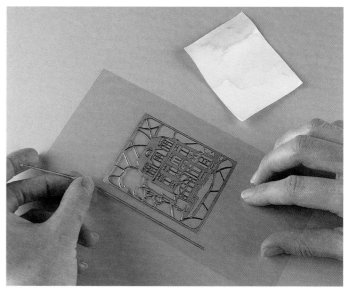

3 Let the watercolor painting dry. With a ruler, measure the size of the house outline sticker. Pencil in the measurements onto the watercolor painting or hold the outline sticker over the painting and then trim the background so that it fits exactly behind the outline sticker.

4 To frame the house outline sticker, remove one strip at a time from the border sticker sheet and position each strip on the acetate about ½ in (1 cm) from the house sticker. When all four borders are in place, cut around the border.

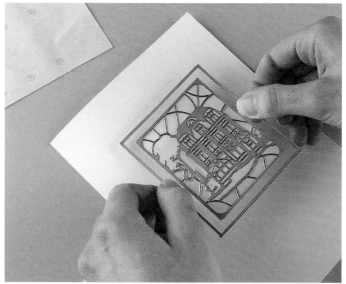

5 Use glue dots or a small amount of glue on the back of the acetate to attach it to the watercolor background.

6 Score the second 11¾ x 8¼-in (30 x 21-cm) white watercolor card down the center lengthwise, using the ruler and the embossing tool, and fold over. Centrally position the design on the front of the card and stick down using a little more glue. ■

Pretty parcel

Everyone should have a little glitter in their life, especially around birthdays and Christmas. This sparkly card is the perfect accompaniment to a gift. You could also accessorize with a matching gift tag to complete the picture.

YOU WILL NEED

Parcel and bow double-sided sticker
  1½ x 1½ in (4.5 x 4.5 cm)
Scissors
Small piece of spare white card
Dark blue and silver glitter

8¼ x 5¾-in (21 x 15-cm) silver holographic
  card
8¼ x 5¾-in (21 x 15-cm) blue sparkle card
8¼ x 5¾-in (21 x 15-cm) duck egg blue
  pearl card
Pencil
Guillotine

3-D foam squares
11¾ x 8¼-in (30 x 21-cm) white card
Ruler
Embossing tool
Glue stick

1 Using a pair of scissors, cut out the parcel and bow motif from the rest of the designs on the sheet. Peel off the protective backing sheet and place it sticky side down onto the piece of spare white card. Press down and gently remove the backing sheet to reveal the design, which will have a sticky surface.

2 Sprinkle the dark blue glitter over the surface of the design starting at the top and leaving some areas uncovered, then sprinkle the silver glitter toward the bottom of the design. Tap off the excess glitter and return it to the pot. **steps 3–6 ▶**

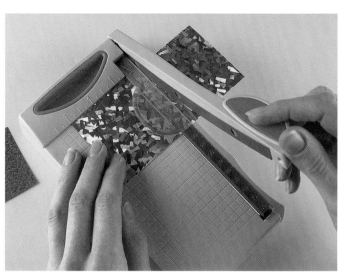

3 Cut around the parcel, leaving a small border of white card showing.

4 Cut a 3-in (7-cm) square from the silver holographic card, a 2½-in (6-cm) square from the blue sparkle card, and a 2-in (5-cm) square from the duck egg blue pearl card, using the pencil to mark the measurements and the guillotine to ensure a straight and even cut.

5 Place 3-D foam glue pads onto the back of the parcel, then remove the backing from the foam pads and centrally position the parcel onto the duck egg blue pearl card.

6 Cut the white card to 8 x 6 in (20 x 15 cm) and score it down the center lengthwise, using the ruler and the embossing tool, and then fold over. Glue the silver holographic square onto the front of the white card, followed by the blue sparkle square, and the duck egg blue pearl square with the parcel. ■

TIP When using scissors for cutting out detail, always hold them at a 90-degree angle from your body and turn the image you are cutting rather than the scissors. This allows you to see the image better, ensuring fewer mistakes and a closer finish.

Tulip time

These tulips look spectacular adorning this pyramid card. Write your greeting message on the inside of the card and send it flat for the recipient to fold into an upright pyramid.

YOU WILL NEED

Scissors
11¾ x 8¼-in (30 x 21-cm) pale
   lemon card
Pencil
Cutting mat
Craft knife

Ruler
Embossing tool
Six 3¼-in (8-cm) high 3-D paper
   tulip stickers
Fifteen 1¼-in (3-cm) high tulip stickers

1 Photocopy the pyramid template on page 123 and cut it out. Place the template onto the pale lemon card, trace around the outline with a pencil, and cut it out carefully using scissors.

2 Using the template as a guide, lightly mark the fold lines and slit for the tab with a pencil. Carefully cut the slit with a craft knife, placing the cutting mat underneath to protect your work surface. Score along the fold lines using the ruler and the embossing tool. Leave a small space at the tip of the pyramid unscored.

3 Place the pyramid card right side up on your work surface and gently remove the large tulip stickers from the backing sheet. Position them as if they are growing from the bottom edge of the card, two per triangle.

4 Finally, remove the smaller tulips from the backing sheet and complete the design by adding five per triangle at the base of the larger tulips. ■

Bonny bib

This unique card will bring a smile to the face of any new mom. Silver peel-offs edge the card for a perfect finish. Pastel cards work equally well for this design.

YOU WILL NEED

11¾ x 8¼-in (30 x 21-cm) white card
Ruler
Embossing tool
Pencil
Scissors
Eraser

Silver decorative outline stickers
Silver sticker dots
Pricking tool
Baby girl stickers to include an umbrella, star, teddy bear, and duck

1 Using the ruler and the embossing tool, score the 11¾ x 8¼-in (30 x 21-cm) white card down the center lengthwise and fold over. Using the bib template on page 124, trace the outline of the shape in pencil onto the folded card, making sure that the design is placed at the edge of the fold. Cut out the design and erase any pencil marks.

2 To decorate the neck edge of the bib, peel off the decorative outline sticker from the backing sheet and stick it close to the edge, as shown in the picture.

3 The delicate detail around the bib is created using tiny sticker dots. Use the pricking tool to pick up each individual dot and place it in position.

4 Finally, gently remove the premade baby sticker from the backing sheet and position it on the front of the card just below the neck edge. ■

3-D butterflies

This three-dimensional holographic card really stands out from the crowd. Combine silver outline stickers with holographic outline stickers and textured card for perfect results.

YOU WILL NEED

Red holographic sticker
   7½ x 7½ in (9 x 9 cm)
Sheet of acetate
Scissors

8¼ x 5¾-in (21 x 15-cm) gold card
Ribbler
Glue dots
White 11¾ x 8¼-in (30 x 21-cm) card

Ruler
Embossing tool
Three butterfly outline stickers

1 Carefully remove the red holographic sticker from the backing sheet and position it onto the piece of acetate. Cut the acetate to the size of the sticker.

2 Use the ribbler to create a corrugated effect on the gold card. Hold the tool in one hand and feed the card between the rollers. Turn the handle and watch the ribbled card come out the other end. Cut the ribbled card so that it is slightly larger than the red sticker. **steps 3–6 ▶**

3 Centrally glue down the acetate with the sticker onto the ribbled card using glue dots placed on the back of the sticker.

4 Cut a 9 x 4½-in (22 x 11-cm) rectangle from the white card and score it down the center lengthwise, using the ruler and the embossing tool, and fold over. Position the ribbled card and sticker on the front of the white card and glue in place.

5 You will need three butterfly stickers to achieve a 3-D butterfly. Remove the first butterfly from the backing sheet and fold it in half, sticky side out. Do the same with the second butterfly and place the sticky side of the left wing of butterfly two on the sticky side of the right wing of butterfly one so that the wings overlap each other. Repeat the same process for butterfly three but stick its right wing to the left wing of butterfly one.

6 Open up the butterfly and, taking care not to let the two remaining sticky wings come into contact with each other, place them onto the center of the holographic sticker and press down to stick into place. ■

Christmas bauble

This is a Christmas card with a difference. The velvet bauble sticker is beautifully displayed when hanging freely in the aperture of the card. Simple and quicker than you would think to make, this card is perfect for sending out to family and friends over the holidays.

YOU WILL NEED

Scissors
11¾ x 8¼-in (30 x 21-cm) white card
Pencil
Cutting mat
Craft knife

Ruler
Embossing tool
Two red flock bauble stickers
Red thread
Leftovers from outline stickers in gold

Pricking tool
Gold border sticker
Glue stick
Hole punch or eyelet maker
Gold ribbon

1 Photocopy the bauble template on page 124 and cut it out. Place the template onto the white card and trace around the outline with a pencil. Fold the card in half along Fold 1 and cut out the outline. Open the card and place it flat on the cutting mat. Cut out the aperture with the craft knife. Fold the card over again and trace around the cut aperture so that it is transferred onto the other side of the card. Cut it out, using the craft knife. With the ruler and the embossing tool, score along Folds 2 and 3 and fold over.

2 To make the bauble, remove the first bauble sticker from the backing sheet, and place it onto your work surface sticky side up. Position the red thread onto the bauble, making sure there is sufficient thread coming out of the top of the bauble with which to hang it. Remove the second bauble and place it on top of the first bauble so that the sticky sides are together. **steps 3–6 ▶**

3 Using the small elements that are left over when outline stickers have been used for another design, decorate both sides of the bauble. Use a pricking tool to pick up very small pieces.

4 Remove the gold border sticker from the backing sheet and position it around both the front and back apertures of the card.

5 Open the card flat and, with the wrong side uppermost, attach the end of the red thread to the card using a small piece of white paper and glue.

6 Fold the card over and make a small hole at the top (one on either side) using a hole punch or an eyelet maker, and thread the gold ribbon through both holes, securing with a pretty bow. ■

Bouquet of flowers

Send this beautiful bouquet of flowers as a perfect get-well-soon card or simply just to say hello. Definitely a card for the cherished recipient to treasure.

YOU WILL NEED

11³⁄₄ x 8¹⁄₄-in (30 x 21-cm) white card
Ruler
Embossing tool
Decorative scissors (Victorian wide)
8¹⁄₄ x 5³⁄₄-in (21 x 15-cm) lemon diamond
    pattern vellum

Pricking tool
8¹⁄₄ x 5³⁄₄-in (21 x 15-cm) purple striped
    vellum
Iris and daffodil bouquet rubdown
    4¹⁄₂-in (11-cm) high
Popsicle stick

Scissors
Glue dots
Gold ribbon

1 Cut the 11³⁄₄ x 8¹⁄₄-in (30 x 21-cm) white card to 8 x 6 in (20 x 15 cm). Score it down the center lengthwise, using the ruler and the embossing tool, and fold over. Using the decorative edge scissors, align the top edge of the scissors with the front edge of the card and trim the card to leave a fancy finish.

2 Cut the lemon vellum to fit the front of the white card and edge the right-hand side with the decorative edge scissors. Using the border made by the decorative scissors as a guide, make a continuous row of small holes using the pricking tool on both the white card and the yellow vellum.
steps 3–6 ▶

3 Cut out the iris and daffodil rubdown from the backing sheet. Remove the backing sheet and position the rubdown onto a piece of purple striped vellum. Rub a Popsicle stick firmly over the surface of the rubdown to release it from the carrier sheet and then gently peel off the carrier sheet.

4 Using small scissors, carefully trim around the floral design to leave a small border of purple.

5 Using glue dots, stick the yellow vellum onto the front of the white card followed by the purple vellum with the floral sticker.

6 Tie a small bow from the gold ribbon and position it over the stems of the flowers, using a glue dot to hold it in place. ■

3 Cut the red pearl card to a 4½-in (11-cm) square using the guillotine and position a 4-in (10-cm) square of white card in the middle of the red card and glue in place. Glue both cards onto the front of the blank greeting card set aside from Step 1, ensuring they are positioned centrally.

4 To make the eyelet holes in each of the four corners, position the card face up on the eyelet mat and place the eyelet punch in one corner, hold the tool at its base, and, keeping it vertical, hit the top of the hole punch hard with the hammer—once should be enough. Repeat on all corners.

5 Turn the card over. Position the eyelets one at a time, eyelet side down on the mat. Position the holes directly over each eyelet so that the barrel of the eyelet shows through the card. Put the eyelet setter into the eyelet, and, holding it close to the card, hit it sharply with the hammer. The idea is to flatten the back of the eyelet to secure it in place.

6 Assemble the card by placing the mounted rub-on in the center of the front of the card and glue it in position. ■

TIP When making holes for eyelets, work over an eyelet mat because cutting mats can get damaged.

Mini card and envelope

Try something a little different with this cute envelope card. It's amazing how a simple paper folding technique can look so effective, using handmade mulberry paper for extra effect. Why not create a matching gift tag and make your gift wrapping something to remember.

YOU WILL NEED

8¼ x 5¾-in (21 x 15-cm) lilac card
Ruler
Embossing tool

Scissors
Sheet of lilac handmade mulberry paper
Paintbrush

Glue stick
Pre-embossed tulip design, large and small
Sticker maker

1 Turn the 8¼ x 5¾-in (21 x 15-cm) lilac card over so the wrong side of the card is uppermost. Using the ruler and the embossing tool, score down the center lengthwise and fold over. Set aside. To make the miniature envelope, cut a 4 x 8-in (10 x 20-cm) rectangle from the lilac mulberry paper and fold it in half lengthwise and crease the fold. Now fold the paper in half vertically and crease the second fold. The original piece of paper has now been quartered.

2 Position the folded edge of the handmade paper closest to your body and unfold the second fold. Fold the top left and right corners into the center, making sure the two triangles meet. **steps 3–6 ▶**

3 Fold the point over so that it touches the bottom folded edge. Fold the two remaining edges into the center, as in the previous step. Now fold the point over toward the bottom, about 1/2 in (1 cm) above the first point.

4 Make a mini card from the remaining piece of white card. Cut it to a 3 x 4-in (7.5 x 10-cm) rectangle, fold it in half lengthwise, and set it aside. Prepare the mulberry paper for mounting onto the mini card. Place the ruler on the paper, run a damp paintbrush down the side of the ruler, and then tear along the line to achieve soft-feathered edges. The paper should be slightly smaller than the white card.

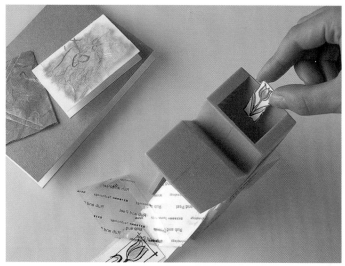

5 Place the mulberry paper on the front of the mini white card and glue it in place. Position the mini envelope and mini card onto the front of the main greeting card at an angle and glue them in place.

6 To make the stickers from the pre-embossed tulip images, pull the adhesive tape until it appears out the bottom of the sticker maker. Drop the images face up into the sticker maker and pull the tape through the machine until the images appear on the tape. Tear the tape and rub gently over the top film before peeling it off to expose the stickers. Remove the stickers from the backing sheet and place them on the front of the mini card and envelope. ■

Wedding celebration

Why not make a card the bride and groom will cherish forever in celebration of their special day. There are so many wedding-themed outline stickers that it is often difficult to choose just the one design. Coupled with the elegant lace effect down the side, this card is a perfect design for a modern or traditional wedding.

YOU WILL NEED

8¼ x 5¾-in (21 x 15-cm) pink card
Ruler
Embossing tool
Lacé template 5 x 2 in (13 x 2.5 cm)
Low tack masking tape

Cutting mat
Craft knife
Glue dots
Silver wedding cake outline sticker
    3 x 2 in (7 x 4.5 cm)

8¼ x 5¾-in (21 x 15-cm) sheet of vellum
Pink gel pen
Scissors
Background cards in silver, pink, and white
Glue stick

1 Turn the 8¼ x 5¾-in (21 x 15-cm) pink card over so that the wrong side is uppermost. Score down the center of the card using the ruler and the embossing tool and fold over. Place the open card flat on your work surface and position the lacé template on the right-hand edge of the front of the card, holding it in place with low tack masking tape. Place a cutting mat beneath the card and, using the lacé template as a guide and a sharp craft knife, cut into the card following the lines of the template, making sure that the craft knife cuts right into the corners of the template lines.

2 Carefully remove the lacé template. Hold the card in your hand, right side up. Working from right to left, release the first cut shape and fold it down. Repeat with each of the cut shapes in turn, tucking the triangular points one beneath the other to hold them in place. Use a glue dot to hold the last one down. **steps 3–6** ▶

3 Gently remove the wedding cake outline sticker from the backing sheet and position it onto the piece of vellum.

4 Use the pink gel pen to color in the vellum background behind the outline sticker, taking care to leave some of the vellum background showing through.

5 With a pair of scissors cut around the wedding cake outline sticker, as close to the edge of the sticker as possible. Hold the scissors still as you close the blades and turn the vellum—this will ensure a smooth edge.

6 Cut the background cards to size so that each layer is slightly bigger than the other, starting with the silver, then pink, and finally white. Position the background rectangles centrally on the front of the card and glue each layer down. When working with vellum, stick the background layers down first, layering toward the vellum and sticking the vellum layer last. ■

STENCILS

Seashells 52

Leafy tag 55

Embossed delight 58

Golden parcels 68

Sail away 70

Flower power 72

Spirelli rose 61

Baby boom 64

Geometric squares 66

Sparkly Christmas tree 75

Perfect poppy 78

Birthday purse 81

Stencil techniques

Stenciling is simple, effective, and gives great results. With a multitude of designs and materials readily available, it is possible to achieve a broad range of finishes. Sticky stencils are a new generation of stencils, repositionable and self-adhesive. Because they are made of latex they are very pliable and are suitable to use on both flat and curved surfaces. They can also be used for dry embossing or regular stenciling. Plastic stencils require a thin film of spray adhesive to create a temporary bond with the surface to be stenciled. Metal stencils are not suitable for regular stenciling because the contact between the stencil and the surface is not usually tight enough to stop color bleeding under the stencil, but they are fabulous to use for dry embossing and give a very effective raised finish.

Securing nonmetallic stencils in place

To secure the stencil in place and ensure that when coloring in the color doesn't bleed, it is important to have a tight contact between the stencil and the surface being stenciled. Use spray adhesive to provide a sticky back to the stencil. Place the stencil on a piece of paper and, holding the can approximately 10 in (25 cm) away from the stencil, spray it evenly. Always work in a well-ventilated room when doing this. Place the stencil sticky-side-down on the paper, ready for coloring in.

Coloring stencil designs

There are several ways to color in stencils. The most popular is to use stencil paint or stencil creams. Dab a small amount of paint onto a stencil brush and use a piece of paper towel to remove the excess. Tap the brush lightly onto the stencil and use a clean brush each time you change color. When you have finished coloring in, peel off the stencil and wash it in warm soapy water. You can also use chalks and watercolor paints but take care because the bond between the stencil and the surface must be tight enough to prevent the paint bleeding under the stencil.

Securing metal stencils in place

Metal stencils such as those used for mola cutting, lacé, and silhouette cutting need to be secured to the card with low tack masking tape. Mola cutting differs from silhouette cutting in that a silhouette template is more often a picture rather than a modular design.

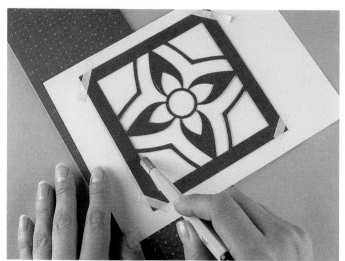

Cutting from metal stencils

Place the secured stencil over a cutting mat to protect your work surface. When cutting with a craft knife, it is important that the blade is sharp so change the blade regularly. Place the knife point as close as possible to the sides of the stencil with the handle vertical and then lower the handle and draw the blade so that it comes into contact with the card.

Securing embossing stencils in place

The most popular use for metal stencils is dry embossing, a simple technique that requires a light box. Secure the metal stencil in place onto the light box with low tack masking tape before you start work.

Embossing technique

With the stencil taped in place, switch on the light box and position the card over the stencil, wrong side uppermost. Use the embossing tool to make indentations in the card. Use the largest, most rounded size tool that fits your stencil to avoid tearing the card (a smaller tool head will be sharper, therefore increasing the risk of tearing the card). Pressing down firmly, draw the tool against the edges of the stencil. When you have completed the stencil's outline, turn the card over to check that the design shows through clearly.

Seashells

These magical foil seashells bring a unique look to your greeting card. Combine them with textured paper to complete the look.

YOU WILL NEED

8¼ x 5¾-in (21 x 15-cm) white card
Three sticky seashell stencils
Adhesive paste
Spatula
8¼ x 5¾-in (21 x 15-cm) sheet of blue metallic foil

Scissors
8¼ x 5¾-in (21 x 15-cm) pearl white card
Ribbler
8¼ x 5¾-in (21 x 15-cm) blue mirror card
8¼ x 5¾-in (21 x 15-cm) aqua blue card

11¾ x 8¼-in (30 x 21-cm) ivory pearl card
Ruler
Embossing tool
Glue stick
3-D foam glue pads

1 Place the three sticky seashell stencils onto the 8¼ x 5¾-in (21 x 15-cm) white card. Rub over using a finger to ensure a good adhesion to the card surface.

2 Apply the adhesive paste generously over the stencils using the spatula. Take time to work back and forth over the stencils to ensure a smooth finish. Because the foil that will be placed over them is so fine, any bumps in the adhesive will show through. Carefully peel away the stencils from the card and wash them in warm soapy water. Let the adhesive dry for about 30 minutes. **steps 3–6 ▶**

3 Lay the blue metallic foil metallic side up over the adhesive. Rub over the foil using your finger to ensure the foil has stuck completely.

4 Slowly peel away the foil from the surface of the adhesive. If any pieces of adhesive are not covered with the foil repeat the process. Using the scissors, cut around the foiled images, leaving a small border around the edges of each shell.

5 To make the backing layer, feed the pearl white card through the ribbler to create a ribbled effect. Cut the ribbled card to a 3-in (7.5-cm) square. Next, cut the blue mirror card to a 3½-in (8.5-cm) square. Finally, cut the piece of aqua blue card to a 4-in (9.5-cm) square.

6 Score the 11¾ x 8¼-in (30 x 21-cm) ivory pearl card down the center lengthwise using the ruler and the embossing tool. To assemble the card, start building up the layers. Stick the aqua blue card to the front of the ivory pearl card, followed by the blue mirror card, and finally the ribbled white card. Place a 3-D foam glue pad on the back of each shell and position over the ribbled card. ■

Leafy tag

Layered handmade papers add an interesting touch to any greeting card. A little simple stenciling in natural colors combined with cord and brads (fasteners) complete the look for a very unusual card.

YOU WILL NEED

Small piece of white card
Sticky leaf stencil 2½ x 2 in (6 x 4.5 cm)
Stencil brush
Stencil paints in green, yellow, and brown
Paper towel
Scissors
Eyelet mat

Eyelet setter
Hammer
White string
8¼ x 5¾-in (21 x 15-cm) handmade mulberry papers in dark green and lime green
Ruler

Paintbrush
8¼ x 5¾-in (21 x 15-cm) pale green card
Embossing tool
Glue stick
Paper brad

1 Place the sticky leaf stencil on a piece of white card large enough to hold the stencil and rub over using your finger to ensure a good adhesion to the card surface. Color in the leaf design with the stencil brush, using a mix of green, yellow, and brown stencil paints. Wipe off any excess paint from the stencil brush with a paper towel. Gently pull the stencil away from the card and let the paint dry before cutting out the tag. Wash the stencil in warm soapy water.

2 Place the tag on the eyelet mat to protect your work surface. Using the eyelet setter, make a hole in the top two corners of the tag. Hold the eyelet setter vertically and hit the top of it firmly with a hammer. **steps 3–6 ▶**

3 Measure a length of white string no more than 3-in (7.5-cm) long. Feed the piece of string through each of the holes made by the eyelet setter and tie off on the front of the tag, making a small knot in each end of the string.

4 Prepare the mulberry paper for tearing. Place the dark green paper on your work surface and run the wet paintbrush along the edge of the ruler. This softens the paper and makes it easier to tear. Gently tear along the wetted line and repeat for the remaining three sides so that you end up with a rectangle 3 x 5 in (8 x 12 cm) in size. Repeat the process on the lime green paper so that you have a rectangle 2½ x 3 in (6.5 x 8 cm) in size.

5 Score the 8¼ x 5¾-in (21 x 15-cm) pale green card down the center lengthwise, using the ruler and the embossing too,l and fold over. Stick the layers of mulberry paper onto the front of the pale green card, mounting the dark green first followed by the lime green.

6 To make the hole for the brad, unfold the card and place the front of it on the eyelet mat. Using the eyelet setter, make a hole in the center of the front of the card, making sure the hole is central and goes through both layers of handmade paper. Push the paper brad through the hole and pull out the legs to secure the brad. Ensure there is sufficient space to allow the string to hang. Hang the tag with the cord over the brad to complete the card. A gift tag on a present completed in the same way would really complement this card. ■

Embossed delight

This card is brought to life by using a light box and embossing tool to create a dry embossed effect. Embossing is simple and effective. To add further dimension, the card is mounted onto acetate and secured in place with eyelets. The cute butterfly tag adds the finishing touch.

YOU WILL NEED

8¼ x 5¾-in (21 x 15-cm) lilac pearl card
Embossing stencil to include leaf, flower,
    bird, butterfly, and square
Light box
Low tack masking tape
Embossing tool
Scissors

Small piece of white card
Glue stick
Sheet of acetate
Eyelet mat
Eyelet setter
Hammer
Four pink eyelets

Ruler
11¾ x 8¼-in (30 x 21-cm) white card
Pencil
Cutting mat
Craft knife

1 Cut the lilac pearl card so that it is slightly larger than the butterfly embossing stencil. Position the stencil onto the light box and secure in place with low tack masking tape. Place the lilac pearl card pearl-side down over the light box and, using the embossing tool, trace around the squares and around the stencil border to create a frame.

2 Emboss the butterfly motif again on a leftover piece of lilac pearl card, using the same technique as before and ensuring the colored side is face down. Emboss a frame around the outside of the butterfly and then cut out. Transfer the tag template on page 125 onto a piece of white card and cut it out. Use the embossing tool to emboss around the border to highlight the design. Glue the lilac butterfly onto the front of the tag, as shown in the final picture. **steps 3–6** ▶

3 Cut the acetate so that it is about 1 in (2.5 cm) larger than the lilac pearl card. To secure the lilac card and acetate together, place the acetate centrally onto the back of the card and make a hole in each corner with the eyelet setter and hammer, making sure to place the eyelet mat underneath to protect your work surface.

4 Turn the card over so that the right side is facing you and hammer in three pink eyelets, leaving out the top right eyelet for now. Now place the tag at the top right-hand corner of the card and secure into place from the front with the remaining pink eyelet.

5 Cut the 11¾ x 8¼-in (30 x 21-cm) white card to 6 x 11 in (15 x 28 cm). Score the card down the center lengthwise, using the ruler and the embossing tool, and fold over. To make the aperture, measure the lilac pearl card and pencil in the measurements onto the front of the card. Add another 1 in (2.5 cm) to the size of the aperture. Cut around the lines using a craft knife, ensuring you place the opened card on the cutting mat.

6 Finally, assemble the card by sticking the acetate onto the back of the front aperture. ■

Spirelli rose

This card combines the beauty of spirelli with the simplicity of stenciling. Spirelli is the term given to the art of winding decorative threads around card shapes to create kaleidoscope patterns. The shapes can be cut by hand, punched out, or bought precut.

YOU WILL NEED

Small piece of white card
Sticky flower stencil 2¹/₂ x 5¹/₂-in (4 x 6-cm)
Stencil paints in red, burgundy, and green
Two stencil brushes
Water pot

Scissors
11³/₄ x 8¹/₄-in (30 x 21-cm) lilac card
Rose metallic thread
Sticky tape
11³/₄ x 8¹/₄-in (30 x 21-cm) white card

Ruler
Embossing tool
8¹/₄ x 5³/₄-in (21 x 15-cm) lilac pearl card
Pencil
Glue stick

1 Place the sticky flower stencil on a piece of white card large enough to hold the stencil. Mix the red and burgundy stencil paints together to create a rich red, adding a small amount of water to the mix. Color in the rose petal using the stencil brush.

2 Using a clean stencil brush, mix a small amount of green paint with a little water. Dab this lightly over the leaves to create a watercolor effect.

3 Once the paint has dried, cut around the flower leaving a small border around the design. **steps 4–7 ▶**

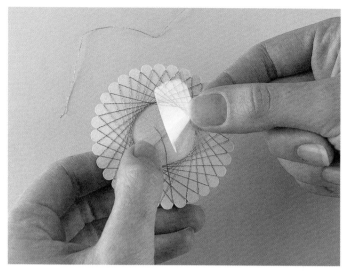

4 Transfer the spirelli template on page 125 onto the piece of lilac card and stick the rose metallic thread to the back of it with a small piece of sticky tape. Turn the shape over and start to wind the thread back and forth, leaving a space of 10 notches between each wind.

5 The pattern will begin to develop quickly as you work. Continue working around, so that each notch has been threaded twice. Once complete, secure the end of the thread at the back with a piece of sticky tape.

6 Score the 11³/₄ x 8¹/₄ in (297 x 210 mm) white card down the center lengthwise, using the ruler and the embossing tool, and fold over. Reproduce the octagonal template on page 125 onto this card, making sure you place one of the sides along the fold of the card. Cut out the octagonal shape.

7 Using the template on page 125, trace and cut out the shape on the lilac pearl card, face down. Position the lilac shape on the front of the white octogonal card and glue it in place. Position the spirelli shape over the center of the lilac shape and glue in place. To finish the card, glue the stenciled flower on the front of the spirelli shape. ■

Baby boom

Bonny in blue or pretty in pink, the choice is yours. A lovely card to give to a new mother, guaranteed to take pride of place and to be cherished for years to come. Follow the instructions for a simple introduction to harmonica folding.

11¾ x 8¼-in (30 x 21-cm) white card
Ruler
Embossing tool
Harmonica fold template
Craft knife

Baby embossing stencil to include pram,
   bottle, heart, duck, and booties
Light box
Low tack masking tape
11¾ x 8¼-in (30 x 21-cm) pearl blue card

Scissors
Striped blue vellum
Glue stick

1 Cut the 11¾ x 8¼-in
(30 x 21-cm) white card to
6 x 12 in (15 x 30 cm). Mark the card
along the longest edge at 3½ in (9 cm)
and then at 7 in (18 cm) and, using the
ruler and the embossing tool, score
vertically along these marks. Fold the
card to the back along the first line and
to the front along the second line.
Open the card flat and line the central
square of the harmonica fold template
vertically along the first fold. Cut the
three sides of the central square with a
craft knife. When the card is folded
closed, this square will stand out.

2 Place the heart embossing
template onto the light box and
secure it in place with low tack
masking tape. Place the back of the
white card face down over the heart
embossing template and, using the
embossing tool, randomly emboss the
hearts down the outer edge.

3 Cut a 5½ x 2-in (13.5 x 5-cm)
rectangle from the 11¾ x 8¼-in
(30 x 21-cm) pearl blue card. Emboss
the pram in the center of the card,
then the bottle at an angle at the top,
the booties at the bottom, and
randomly placed hearts. Cut another
rectangle from the pearl blue card
1½ x 2 in (3.5 x 4.5 cm) in size. Place
it onto the duck stencil face down and
emboss using the embossing tool.

4 Cut out a 6 x 2½-in (15 x 6-cm)
rectangle from the striped blue
vellum. Glue it to the front left of the
card, as shown in the picture.

5 Position the embossed long blue
strip over the vellum and stick it
in place with glue. Finally, glue down
the embossed duck on the right-hand
side of the card. ■

Geometric squares

Lacé in French means linked together. This refers to the cutting and folding under of the paper flaps on a lacé card. Using duo card makes the effect even more striking. Lacé is detailed and intricate but, with the proper instructions, is very easy to achieve.

YOU WILL NEED

11¾ x 8¼-in (30 x 21-cm) duo red and green card
Pencil
Ruler
Cutting mat

Craft knife
Lacé template 6 x 1¾ in (15 x 4 cm)
Low tack masking tape
Lacé craft knife
Glue dots

Gold peel-off strips
11¾ x 8¼-in (30 x 21-cm) cream card
Embossing tool
Glue stick

1 Cut a 6 x 2-in (15 x 5-cm) rectangle from the duo red and green card. Mark a border ½ in (0.5 cm) inside the rectangle and cut it out over the cutting mat using the craft knife. Keep the frame aside because you will need it for Step 4.

2 Place the lacé template over the two-tone card, red side up. Secure in place onto the cutting mat using low tack masking tape. Follow the template, cutting the design out with the lacé craft knife. Take care when cutting out because the design is quite intricate. Start each cut with the point of the blade pushed into the card and the knife handle vertical, then lower the angle to 45 degrees and draw the knife through the guidelines.

3 Turn the card over and fold back the cut lines. Fold back every other cut line, creating a two-tone effect of red and green. If the lines don't stay stuck down just by folding back, use glue dots to secure them in place.

4 Take the cut-out frame from Step 1 and turn it over so that the green side is uppermost. Stick the gold peel-off strips centrally around all four sides of the frame, ensuring that the corners are joined and the ends are finished neatly.

5 Cut the 11¾ x 8¼-in (30 x 21-cm) cream card to 8 x 8 in (20 x 20 cm). Score the card down the center lengthwise, using the ruler and the embossing tool, and fold over. Apply some glue to the back of the red lacé strip and stick it down on the front of the card. Finally, stick down the frame, which should fit perfectly around the card. The cream background will show through the folded over lacé strips. ■

Golden parcels

Keep colours to a simple gold and white for a clean, minimalist look. The parcels have been stenciled for speed and the whole card layered. If you need to make a birthday card in a hurry, this is the perfect solution.

YOU WILL NEED

Spare piece of white card
Sticky parcel stencil 1 x 1 in (2.5 x 2.5 cm)
Gold stencil cream
Cotton bud
Scissors
11¾ x 8¼-in (30 x 21-cm) white card

Ruler
Embossing tool
8¼ x 5¾-in (21 x 15-cm) gold card
8¼ x 5¾-in (21 x 15-cm) gold holographic
  card
Glue stick
3-D foam glue pads

1 Place the sticky parcel stencil on a piece of white card large enough to hold the stencil and rub over it with your finger to ensure a bond between the stencil and the card. Use a cotton bud to shade in the stencil with the gold stencil cream. Carefully peel off the stencil from the card and make two more parcels in the same way.

2 Once the parcels are dry, cut them out, leaving a small frame around the edges. Cut out an 8-in (20-cm) square from the 11¾ x 8¼-in (30 x 21-cm) white card. Score the card down the center, using the ruler and the embossing tool, and fold over.

3 Cut out three squares slightly larger than the size of the cut-out parcel squares from the gold card. On the gold holographic card, measure a rectangle 1½ x 6½ in (3 x 16 cm) in size and cut it out. Stick it centrally onto the front of the white card.

4 To assemble the card, stick the parcels onto the gold squares. Place a 3-D foam glue pad on each corner of the back of the gold parcels and mount them at an equal distance apart onto the gold holographic strip. ■

Sail away

This is the perfect card for a man! Shadow silhouette cutting, using a metal stencil template, conjures up images of lazy days on the sea as with this simple yet effective sailboat card.

YOU WILL NEED

8¼ x 5¾-in (21 x 15-cm) white card
Ruler
Embossing tool
Cutting mat
Sailing boat stencil 5 x 5½ in (13 x 6 cm)
Low tack masking tape

Pencil
Craft knife
Stencil brushes
Decorating chalks in blue, green, yellow, and red
Fixative

1 Score the 8¼ x 5¾-in (21 x 15-cm) white card down the center lengthwise, using the ruler and the embossing tool, and fold over. Make sure you work over the cutting mat to protect your work surface. Position the sailing boat stencil onto the front of the card, securing it in place with low tack masking tape.

2 There are two ways to cut out this design. If you are a beginner, trace the outline of the design using a sharp pencil. Make sure you trace as close to the stencil as possible, then remove the tape and stencil from the card and cut along the lines using the craft knife.

3 If you are more experienced, you can cut out the design against the stencil directly, making sure you keep the craft knife blade as close to the edge of the stencil as possible.

4 Once the stencil has been cut out, open up the card and place it flat on your work surface lined with a sheet of scrap paper. Color in the waves, the hull, the sails, and the clouds using stencil brushes and decorating chalks. Use a clean brush each time you change color. Finally, fix the colors in place with a light spray of fixative. ■

Flower power

Mola cutting has traditionally been used in textiles. Layers of different fabrics are laid on top of each other, then lines are stitched through to create patterns. The layers are then cut into and peeled away to produce beautiful patchwork. This technique has been adapted for card making with amazing results.

YOU WILL NEED

Two sheets 11¾ x 8¼-in (30 x 21-cm) white
   card
Scissors
Ruler
Embossing tool
Mola template 4 x 4 in (10 x 10 cm)

Low tack masking tape
Cutting mat
Craft knife
11¾ x 8¼-in (30 x 21-cm) sheet of
   red paper

Sheet of silver border stickers
Glue stick
8¼ x 5¾-in (21 x 15-cm) blue
   holographic card

1 Cut out a 5-in (13-cm) square from one of the 11¾ x 8¼-in (30 x 21-cm) sheets of white card. From the other sheet, cut a rectangle measuring 5 x 10 in (13 x 26 cm). Score the card down the center lengthwise, using the ruler and the embossing tool, and fold over.

2 Unfold the card and place the mola template on the front of it, securing it with low tack masking tape. Place the card on the cutting mat and cut around the shapes using a craft knife. Repeat on the square piece of white card. **steps 3–6 ▶**

3 Use a pair of scissors or a guillotine to cut red paper strips ½-in wide (1-cm) and trim them with the silver border stickers. Make sure you cut enough to go all the way around the frames of the two mola embellishments.

4 Glue the red strips in place onto the two mola embellishments, cutting the corners at a 45-degree angle for a really professional finish.

5 Cut the blue holographic card so that it is slightly larger than the mola template. Position the front of the card featuring the mola embellishment onto the blue holographic card and glue in place from the back.

6 Diagonally position the second mola embellishment onto the front of the card and secure in place with glue. Trim the corners so that they are flush with the sides of the card. ■

Sparkly Christmas tree

If you can't have glitter at Christmas, then when can you have it? Try this perfect last-minute card idea. Quick and easy stenciling achieves instant results.

YOU WILL NEED

Spare piece of white card
Sticky Christmas tree stencil
  2 x 1½ in (5 x 4 cm)
Green pigment-based ink pad
Silver glitter

Scissors
8¼ x 5¾-in (21 x 15-cm) green
  metallic card
8¼ x 5¾-in (21 x 15-cm) green
  velvet card

Glue stick
8¼ x 5¾-in (21 x 15-cm) white card
Ruler
Embossing tool
Red glitter glue

1 Place the Christmas tree stencil on a piece of white card large enough to hold the stencil. Rub over it with your finger to ensure a good adhesion to the card surface.

2 Stamp the green ink pad onto the stencil. It is important to use a pigment-based pad because the ink needs to remain wet while you sprinkle glitter onto it. Make sure the stencil is completely covered with the ink. **steps 3–6 ▶**

3 Carefully peel off the stencil and wash it in warm soapy water. While the ink is still wet, sprinkle it generously with the silver glitter. Tap off the excess glitter and return it to the pot. Set aside to dry.

4 When the Christmas tree design is dry, cut it out around the border using a pair of scissors. Round off the corners for a softer, less formal finish.

5 Cut the green metallic card so that it is 1 in (2.5 cm) larger than the Christmas tree medallion. Next, cut out the green velvet card so that it is ½ in (1 cm) larger than the green metallic card. Stick the medallion onto the metallic card and then stick the metallic card onto the velvet card.

6 Score the 8¼ x 5¾-in (21 x 15-cm) white card down the center lengthwise, using the ruler and the embossing tool, and fold over. Stick the matted three layers on the front of the card. Finish off the design by squeezing a small amount of red glitter glue on top of the tree. ■

Perfect poppy

Try your hand at shading through a stencil to create this bright and fresh card. You can achieve a fabulous result using acrylic paints. There are many other methods of coloring in stencils, all of which are described on page 50.

YOU WILL NEED

Plastic poppy stencil 4 x 1½ in (10 x 4 cm)
Repositionable poppy stencil adhesive
Spare piece of white card
Stencil paints in red, yellow, and green
Stencil brush
Paper towel

Scissors
Pencil
Ruler
8¼ x 5¾-in (21 x 15-cm) orange card
Ribbler
8¼ x 5¾-in (21 x 15-cm) yellow card

11¾ x 8¼-in (30 x 21-cm) white card
Embossing tool
Glue stick
3-D foam glue pads

1 To ensure the paint does not bleed beneath the stencil, spray it with repositionable stencil adhesive before positioning it, adhesive side down, onto a piece of white card large enough to hold the stencil. Make sure you work in a well-ventilated room. If the stencil is one of the new generation of sticky stencils, you can work without the spray adhesive and place the stencil straight onto the card, rubbing over it with your finger to ensure a good adhesion to the card surface.

2 Mix a small amount of red and yellow stencil paint together and dab it onto the poppy petals with the stencil brush. Wipe off the excess paint onto a piece of paper towel before applying the paint to the stencil. **steps 3–6 ▶**

3 To color in the leaves, start with a little green on the stencil brush, but pick up a small amount of yellow, to brighten the green. This will ensure that the leaves look really fresh. To complete the flower head, fill in the center with a small amount of dark green paint. Set aside to dry and wash your stencil brushes in warm soapy water.

4 Cut out the poppy picture leaving a frame around the poppy. You may want to pencil in the frame first to ensure a straight, even cut.

5 Feed the orange card through the ribbler. Turn the handle and watch the corrugated card come out the other end and then cut the card so that it is slightly larger than the white poppy card. Cut out a rectangle of yellow card slightly larger than the ribbled card so that it will show when placed beneath the orange rectangle.

6 Cut the 11¾ x 8¼ in (297 x 210 mm) white card to an 8-in (20-cm) square. Score it down the center using the ruler and the embossing tool and fold over. To assemble the card, glue the yellow card onto the front of the white card. Apply 3-D foam glue pads to the ribbled card and poppy picture and stick each layer down in place starting with the yellow card, followed by the ribbled card, and finally the poppy picture.

Birthday purse

Try this great card idea, which is perfect for an 18th or 21st birthday celebration.
Vary the color scheme to suit your recipient's preferences.

YOU WILL NEED

11¾ x 8¼-in (30 x 21-cm) white card
Pencil
Scissors
11¾ x 8¼-in (30 x 21-cm) pale lemon card
Eraser

Craft knife
Cutting mat
Metal ruler
Embossing stencil to include
    flower and bow designs

Embossing tool
Light box
6-in (15-cm) orange gingham ribbon
Glue dots

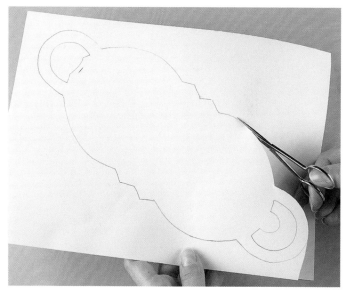

1 Transfer the purse template on page 125 onto the
11¾ x 8¼-in (30 x 21-cm) white card and cut it out. This
template can be used again should you want to make this
card for another occasion, so make sure you save it. Using
the template you have cut out from the white card, trace the
outline carefully onto the reverse side of the pale lemon card.

2 Cut out the handbag shape and erase any pencil
marks. Cut the slit and the tab using the craft knife,
ensuring you place the card on the cutting mat first to
protect your work surface. **steps 3–6 ▶**

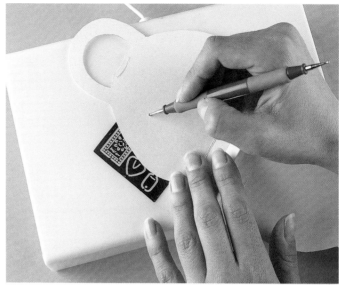

3 On the reverse side of the card, score the base of the purse along all five fold lines using the metal ruler and the embossing tool to create the folds that will help the card stand up.

4 Place the flower and bow embossing stencil over the light box and position the purse card with the lemon side facing down over the stencil. Use the embossing tool to trace the flower design across the front and back of the card. After you have embossed a few flowers lift the card to check how the design is taking shape. Emboss the bow just below the handle using the same method.

5 To make the knot, take the gingham ribbon and make each end into a loop. Hold one loop in each hand and cross over the two loops. Fold the front loop over the back loop and pass it through the hole in the middle, back to the front. Pull both loops to tighten the bow. Adjust the symmetry of the bow by pulling the tails until they are even.

6 To finish off the card, attach the bow to the front of the card with a glue dot placed underneath the knot. Slot the tab in the slit and fold it over to close the card. You can write your message on the inside of the card. ■

STAMPS

Gentleman's relish 88

Golden daisies 91

Let it snow 94

Musical notes 104

Frosty winter tree 107

Balloons galore 110

Delightful daisy tags 96

Beautiful butterflies 99

Enameled flower 102

Enameled heart 113

Sunflowers and butterflies 116

A dalliance with dragonflies 119

Stamping techniques

Rubber-stamping is the stepping stone for many different design elements. Accomplish rubber-stamping and the card-making world is your oyster. When rubber stamping, it is important to work with the correct ink. Use a dye-based ink pad for basic rubber stamping and a pigment-based ink pad for embossing.

BASIC RUBBER STAMPING

Inking the stamp

Lightly tap the dye-based ink pad onto the face of the rubber stamp so that it is evenly coated with ink. Don't rub the pad against the stamp as the ink may smudge the design.

Stamping the image

Work on a flat, stable surface and place the stamp face down onto your chosen support. Press down along the whole surface of the stamp with your fingers to transfer the ink to the paper or card, ensuring you do not rock the stamp: this may cause the image to blur. Lift the stamp off cleanly to reveal the image.

EMBOSSING

Embossing a stamped image

Work with a pigment-based ink pad because the ink will stay wet long enough to sprinkle with embossing powder. Lightly tap the stamp with the pad so that it is evenly coated with ink. Make sure the ink does not get onto the edges of the stamp. Stamp the image onto your chosen support.

Applying the embossing powder

Work over a piece of scrap paper and sprinkle the wet ink with embossing powder. Tap off the excess onto the scrap of paper and return the powder to the pot. You will have to work quite quickly so that the ink does not dry before you apply the powder to it.

Brushing off excess powder

Every little speck of embossing powder will show when the image is heated. Use a small, clean, dry paintbrush to brush off any unwanted powder that remains after tapping off.

Using the heat gun

Heat the embossed image with the heat gun, holding the gun about 6 in (15 cm) away from the image. Make sure you keep the gun moving so that the paper does not scorch.

DOUBLE EMBOSSING

Inking the paper

When using more than one layer of embossing powder (a technique called double embossing), take a pigment-based ink pad and press it onto a piece of card, using the entire surface area of the ink pad.

Stamping the image

While the powder is molten and hot, press the stamp onto the wet embossing powder. Hold the stamp still for a few seconds and remove. Take care at this stage because the hot powder can burn.

Covering with embossing powder

While the ink is still wet, sprinkle the inked paper with embossing powder and tap off the excess, returning it to the pot. Heat the powder with a heat gun and, while the powder is still hot and slightly molten, sprinkle a second layer of embossing powder and heat again. The powder will melt and change color more quickly the second time.

Cutting out the image

Leave the embossing powder to dry for 10 minutes before cutting out the image. Do not leave it to dry for too long, however, because the embossing powder can harden and crack.

Gentleman's relish

Making interesting cards for male friends or relatives isn't always easy. This shirt design card is ideal for any celebratory occasion such as a birthday, retirement, or even a new job. To ensure a perfect looking card, simply coordinate the background colors and shirt colors to match.

YOU WILL NEED

11¾ x 8¼-in (30 x 21-cm) bright
   blue paper
Scissors
Glue stick

11¾ x 8¼-in (30 x 21-cm) pale blue paper
Black dye-based ink pad
Tie rubber stamp 2 in (5 cm)
Spare piece of white card

11¾ x 8¼-in (30 x 21-cm) white card
Ruler
Embossing tool

1 Start by making the shirt. Cut a 8 x 4-in (21 x 10-cm) rectangle from the bright blue paper. Fold the paper in half lengthwise and crease the fold. Open up the piece of paper ready for Step 2.

2 Place the piece of paper flat on your work surface. Fold the bottom of the paper 2½ in (6.5 cm) up and crease the fold. Unfold the paper again.

3 Fold both the long sides so that each edge touches the center fold line created in Step 1. Working from the fold line created in Step 2, fold out the right corner diagonally to make a wing. Repeat with the left corner. The diagonal lines should measure approximately 2½ in (6.5 cm).
steps 4–8 ▶

4 With the wings at the bottom and facing you, fold the wings up 2½ in (6.5 cm) so that they are in the middle of the shirt. Crease the bottom fold.

5 To make the collar fold, cut along the shoulder line from each side ½ in (1.5 cm) into the middle. Take the top outside corners of the collar and fold them diagonally to meet in the center.

6 To make the sleeves, cut ¼ in (0.5 cm) of the way up the sleeves following the line of the sides of the shirt. Now cut a small triangle out from that point down to the sleeve opening. To finish the shirt, scoop out the back neck of the shirt collar with a pair of scissors. Glue the shirt collar down.

7 To make the tie, stamp the tie rubber stamp once onto a piece of white card large enough to hold the tie stamp and cut it out carefully with scissors. Cut the pale blue paper in half lengthwise so that it is 8¼ x 5¾ in (21 x 15 cm). Lightly tap the black ink pad onto the tie rubber stamp. Stamp the image diagonally across the pale blue paper, making sure you re-ink the stamp as necessary. Trim ½ in (1.5 cm) off both one long side and one short side so that this piece of paper is slightly smaller than the front of the white greeting card.

8 Score the 11¾ x 8¼-in (30 x 21-cm) white card down the center lengthwise, with the ruler and the embossing tool, and fold over. To assemble the card, centrally stick the stamped pale blue card onto the front of the white card. Next assemble the shirt onto the remaining piece of pale blue card and cut the card to leave a border around the shirt. Finally, stick the bright blue paper beneath the pale blue paper and place the layers onto the stamped pale blue card and stick into place. ■

Golden daisies

These delightful daisies look lovely in yellow. But by changing the color of the backing card and the daisies' color scheme, this card has all the essential elements for any occasion. Quick and easy to make when you need a card in a hurry.

YOU WILL NEED

Spare piece of white card	Heat gun	Embossing tool
Clear or tinted pigment-based ink pad	11¾ x 8¼-in (30 x 21-cm) white card	Yellow fiber tip pen
Daisy stamp with 5 daisies	Ruler	8¼ x 5¾-in (21 x 15-cm) gold holographic
1½ x 3½ in (3 x 9 cm)	Pencil	card
Scissors	Cutting mat	3-D foam glue pads
Silver embossing powder	Craft knife	Glue stick

1 Lightly tap the ink pad against the daisy stamp and stamp the design onto a piece of white card large enough to hold the daisy stamp design. Be careful not to rock the stamp as you press down firmly. Lift the stamp cleanly away from the paper and cut out the stamped image, leaving a small white border around the design. Sprinkle the silver embossing powder over the stamped image. Tap off the excess powder and return it to the pot. Now hold the heat gun 6 in (15 cm) away from the stamped image and heat the powder until it melts.

2 Take the 11¾ x 8¼-in (30 x 21-cm) white card and, using the ruler and pencil, mark out an 8-in (20-cm) square. Place a cutting mat beneath the card and with the ruler and the craft knife cut along the lines. Score down the center of the card, using the ruler and the embossing tool, and fold over. Color in the daisies using a yellow fiber tip pen. Gentle pen strokes look natural. **steps 3–6 ▶**

3 Cut a piece of gold holographic card about ½ in (1.5 cm) larger than the daisy design.

4 To add further dimension to the project, apply 3-D foam glue pads to the back of the stamped daisy image.

5 Position the stamped daisy image over the gold holographic card. The 3-D foam pads will act as glue to hold the image in place. Make sure that everything is level and lined up before sticking down the daisies.

6 Position the holographic gold card with the daisy design horizontally onto the front of the white folded card and glue it in place. ■

Let it snow

This cute snow people stamp has been embellished using glitter. Why not make this your Christmas card and send it to your family and friends. Try different colors for the snow people's hats and scarves and choose different backing layers to create an individual look for each card.

YOU WILL NEED

11¾ x 8¼-in (30 x 21-cm) cerise pink card
Ruler
Pencil
Cutting mat
Craft knife
Embossing tool
Deckle-edge scissors

Black dye-based ink pad
Snow people stamp 1½ x 3½ in
   (4 x 9 cm)
Piece of white card
Gel pens in purple, blue, green,
   pink, and yellow
Scissors

PVA glue
Holographic glitter
8¼ x 5¾-in (21 x 15-cm) mat gold card
Glue stick

1 Using the ruler and pencil measure a rectangle 6 x 12 in (15 x 30 cm) onto the reverse of the 11¾ x 8¼-in (30 x 21-cm) pink card. Cut out the card on a cutting mat using the ruler and the craft knife. Score the card down the center lengthwise, using the ruler and the embossing tool, and fold over. Use the deckle-edge scissors to give a decorative finish to the edges.

2 Lightly tap the black ink pad onto the snow people stamp then stamp the image onto a piece of white card large enough to hold the image. When positioning the stamp onto the white card, make sure that a large enough border of white shows around the edges of the card. Color in the design using the gel pens. Cut out the stamped card, leaving a border around the design.

3 Apply PVA glue to the foreground. While the glue is still wet, sprinkle the holographic glitter over the glue, tap away the excess, and return it to the pot. Let the glue dry for a few minutes before beginning the next stage. Check the bottle for drying times, because they tend to vary between manufacturers.

4 Cut the gold card so that it is about ½ in (1.5 cm) taller and ½ in (1.5 cm) less wide than the stamped card. Assemble the components of the design horizontally onto the front of the card. Stick down the gold card first followed by the white stamped card, as above. ■

Delightful daisy tags

Fresh and fun, this daisy stamp is so pretty you simply have to try it. I have combined tag art with magic mesh to transform the simple lines of the stamp. Give the card to someone who needs a little sunshine in his or her life.

YOU WILL NEED

Double daisy stamp 1¼ x 3¼ in (3 x 8 cm)
Black pigment-based ink pad
11¾ x 8¼-in (30 x 21-cm) white card
Black embossing powder
Heat gun
Fiber tip pens in yellow, green, and orange
Scissors

Two sheets of 11¾ x 8¼-in (30 x 21-cm)
    pale lemon card
Glue stick
Gold sticky tape 1-in (2.5-cm) wide
Self-adhesive yellow magic mesh
Hole punch
White string

11¾ x 8¼-in (30 x 21-cm) bright
    yellow paper
Ruler
Embossing tool
Pencil

1 Lightly tap the black ink pad onto the double daisy stamp. Stamp the design twice on the 11¾ x 8¼-in (30 x 21-cm) white card, re-inking the stamp in the process. Sprinkle the black embossing powder over both of the stamped images. Tap off the excess powder and return it to the pot. Hold the heat gun about 6 in (15 cm) away from the card and heat the embossing powder until it melts, moving the gun continuously so as to not scorch the card. Set aside to dry.

2 Once dry, color in both of the stamped designs using the yellow fiber tip pen for the petals. Use the green fiber tip pen for the daisy centers and the leaves. Use orange to color in the smaller flowers. You can use alternative colors to create an entirely different effect. Carefully cut out both designs. **steps 3–7** ▶

3 Cut a 3½ x 1½-in (9 x 3.5-cm) rectangle from one of the pale lemon cards. Cut a 3¾ x 1½-in (9.5 x 4-cm) rectangle from the white card. Glue the lemon yellow rectangle onto the white one and then centrally glue one of the daisy images from Step 2 over it.

4 Photocopy the tag template on page 126, transfer it onto a piece of white card, and cut it out. Then cut a length of gold sticky tape and position it to one side of the tag, trimming off the excess.

5 Cut a piece of the self-adhesive yellow magic mesh to fit the tag. Allow the mesh to overlap slightly onto the gold tape. Trim any magic mesh excess and glue the second daisy image in place.

6 Using the hole punch, punch a small hole at the top end of the gift tag. Fold the white string in half and thread it through the hole from the back. Take the loose ends and thread these through the loop. Pull tight but make sure not to tear the card.

7 Score the remaining 11¾ x 8¼-in (30 x 21-cm) pale lemon card down the center lengthwise, using the ruler and the embossing tool, and fold over. Cut a 4 x 5½-in (10 x 14.5-cm) rectangle from the bright yellow paper and glue it in the center of the 11¾ x 8¼-in (30 x 21-cm) folded card. Place the tag next. Line the thread up with the top right corner of the bright yellow rectangle and glue in place. Finally, position the second mounted daisy image from Step 5 in the center, toward the bottom of the yellow rectangle, and glue in place. ■

Beautiful butterflies

This is a lovely butterfly stamp and looks especially effective once colored in and cut out. This card is given another dimension by cutting out the background, making the butterflies look as if they are almost fluttering out of the card.

YOU WILL NEED

11¾ x 8¼-in (30 x 21-cm) white card	Black dye-based ink pad	Craft knife
Scissors	Butterflies and flowers stamp	Fiber tip pens in orange, yellow,
Ruler	3 x 3 in (7 x 7 cm)	blue, pink, and black
Embossing tool	Cutting mat	3-D foam glue pads

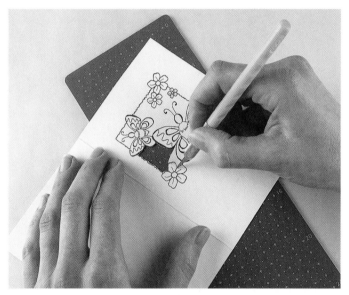

1 Cut the 11¾ x 8¼-in (30 x 21-cm) white card in half lengthwise so that it is 8¼ x 5¾ in (21 x 15 cm) in size. Score the 8¼ x 5¾-in (21 x 15-cm) card down the center lengthwise, using the ruler and the embossing tool, and fold over. Lightly tap the black stamp pad onto the butterfly stamp to cover it evenly with ink. Stamp the image onto the front of the card, taking care not to rock the stamp during the process. Set aside to dry for a few minutes.

2 Open up the card, place it on the cutting mat, and, using the craft knife, cut the detail from around the stamped image to create an aperture in the card. Take extra care when cutting around the delicate antennae of the butterfly. **steps 3–6 ▶**

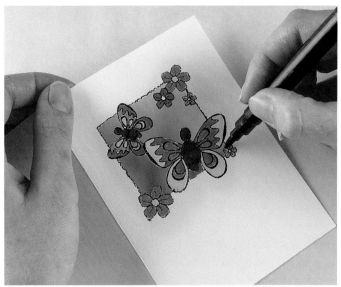

3 Color in the stamped image using the fiber tip pens. An orange, yellow, blue, and pink color scheme has been used here but you can use whichever colors you prefer.

4 To give the colored image a professional finish, color along any exposed edges using a black fiber tip pen. It is important you take care at this stage because you only want black fiber pen along the edges of the aperture.

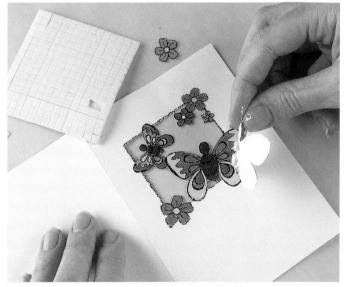

5 To create a three-dimensional effect, stamp the butterfly image twice more onto the remaining piece of white card and set aside to dry. Cut out around the flowers and butterflies of one of the stamped images and color them in using the same color scheme as in Step 3. Cut out one of the smaller flowers from the second stamped image, which will be positioned at the top right-hand corner of the card.

6 To assemble the card, apply 3-D foam glue pads to the back of the cut-out stamped butterflies and flowers. Remove the protective backing sheet from the foam pads and position each of the cut flower shapes over its corresponding shape on the card. Press them in position. Bend the butterflies' wings up slightly and apply 3-D foam glue pads to the back of the bodies and then position them onto the card. Finally, glue the last flower on the top right-hand corner of the white card. ■

Enameled flower

The enameled effect that is created for this card with the glamorous double embossing works best with simple stamp designs. Use as many colored embossing powders as you like to achieve a bright and colorful effect.

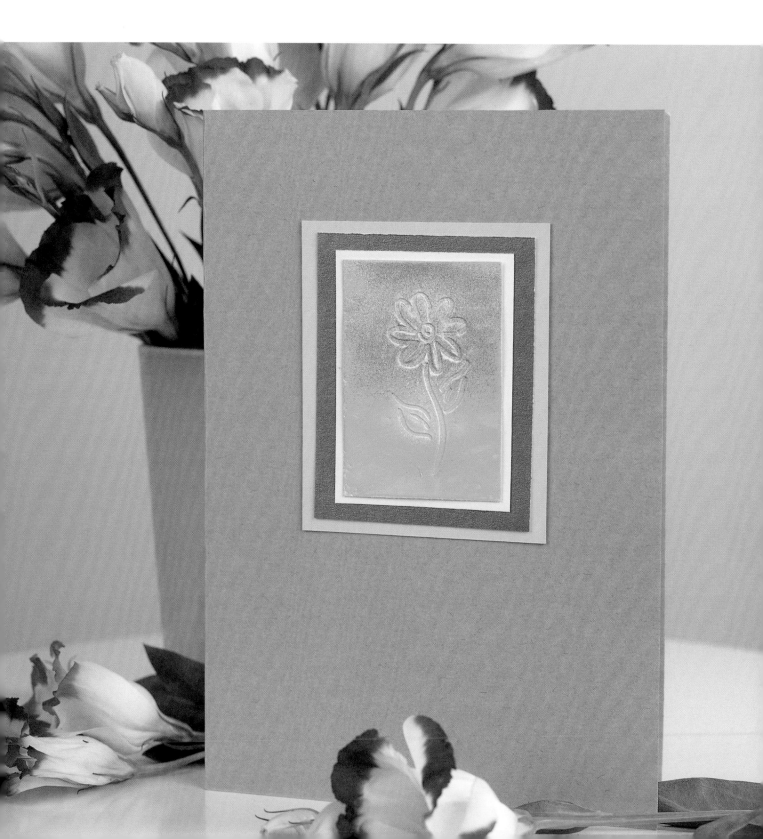

Clear pigment ink pad
Piece of white paper
Daisy stamp 2 x 1¼ in (5 x 3 cm)
Embossing powders in pale green
   and lilac

Heat gun
Scissors
8¼ x 5¾-in (21 x 15-cm) pale green card
8¼ x 5¾-in (21 x 15-cm) lilac pearl card
8¼ x 5¾-in (21 x 15-cm) white card

11¾ x 8¼-in (30 x 21-cm) lilac card
Ruler
Embossing tool
Glue stick

1 To create a double embossed effect, rub the clear ink pad generously over a piece of white card large enough to hold the daisy stamp. While the ink is still wet, cover it with green embossing powder. Tap off the excess and return it to the pot. Holding the heat gun about 6 in (15 cm) away from the card, heat the embossing powder until it melts. Sprinkle the green embossing powder again over the hot melted powder. Tap off the excess and, using the heat gun, heat the powder until it is hot. You will have to work quite quickly to achieve optimum results.

2 Repeat as in Step 1 but this time sprinkle the lilac embossing powder over half the area only. Adding another color will give the final card a more pronounced enameled effect. Take care not to scorch the card with the heat gun.

3 Take the daisy stamp and carefully stamp into the hot molten powder and hold the stamp down for about 20 seconds. Lift cleanly away, ensuring not to rock the stamp during the process. When cool, cut out the stamped image leaving a border around the flower.

4 Cut a 4 x 3-in (10 x 7.5-cm) rectangle from the pale green card, a 3½ x 2½-in (8.5 x 6-cm) rectangle from lilac pearl card, and finally a 2½ x 1½-in (7 x 4.5-cm) rectangle from the white card. Score the 11¾ x 8¼-in (30 x 21-cm) lilac card down the center lengthwise, using the ruler and the embossing tool, and fold over. Mount all the layers of card and stamped image onto the front of the greeting card and glue in place. ■

Musical notes

Create this beautiful musical card for anyone with a love of music. It's perfect if you have tried iris folding before because this is quite intricate, but, if not, follow the simple instructions and you will soon master the technique.

YOU WILL NEED

11³/₄ x 8¹/₄-in (30 x 21-cm) white card
Ruler
Embossing tool
Four sheets of 8¹/₄ x 5³/₄-in (21 x 15-cm)
    white paper
Craft knife

Cutting mat
Low tack masking tape
Pencil
8¹/₄ x 5³/₄-in (21 x 15-cm) black paper
Scissors
Glue dots

Small musical note stamp
Black dye-based ink pad
8¹/₄ x 5³/₄-in (21 x 15-cm) red paper
Sticky tape
Black fine-tipped marker pen

1 Score the 11³/₄ x 8¹/₄-in (30 x 21-cm) white card down the center lengthwise, using the ruler and the embossing tool, and fold over. Replicate the musical note template on page 126 onto a piece of 8¹/₄ x 5³/₄-in (21 x 15-cm) white paper. Hollow out the note using a craft knife. Place the hollowed out template on the front of the opened up 11³/₄ x 8¹/₄-in (30 x 21-cm) white card and secure it in place with low tack masking tape. Place the front of the card over the cutting mat and trace around the note with the pencil or the embossing tool. Remove the template and carefully cut around the tracing with the craft knife to make the aperture.

2 Position the 8¹/₄ x 5³/₄-in (21 x 15-cm) black paper on the back of the aperture so that it covers the top and legs of the musical note. You will have to cut around the base of the note, as shown above, and trim the sides of the black paper to allow the white card to fold over properly. Stick the black paper in place with glue dots. Turn the card over, place it on the cutting mat, and cut away any black paper showing through at the base of the notes with the craft knife. **steps 3–6 ▶**

3 Copy the iris folding template on page 126 onto another piece of 8¼ x 5¾-in (21 x 15-cm) white paper. Position the hollowed out notes over the template, ensuring the card is wrong side up, and secure in place with low tack masking tape.

4 Lightly tap the musical note stamp with the black ink pad and press it onto the 8¼ x 5¾-in (21 x 15-cm) red paper, making sure not to rock the stamp. Re-ink as necessary and repeat until the surface of the paper is covered. Rotate the stamp so that the notes are random. Repeat onto one of the remaining 8¼ x 5¾-in (21 x 15-cm) white paper. Once dry, cut out ¾-in (2-cm) wide strips using the full length of the paper from both the red and white sheets. Fold the strips over lengthwise, ensuring the musical notes are on the outside.

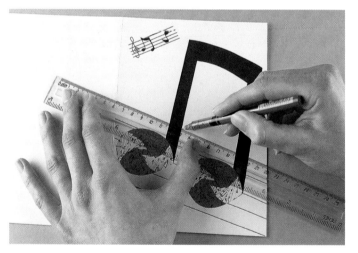

5 To begin iris folding, take a strip of the red stamped folded paper, lay the fold along the edge of Line 1, and secure in place with sticky tape. Next take a strip of the white stamped folded paper, lay the fold along Line 2, and secure in place with sticky tape. Complete the design by alternating the red and white stamped papers and sticking them down along the numbered lines.

6 Stick the last piece of 8¼ x 5¾-in (21 x 15-cm) white paper over the back of the front card to make your card look neat. Turn the card over and, using a black pen draw, some lines so it looks like the musical notes are sitting on a score of music. In the top left-hand corner draw five lines at an angle and a treble clef and two musical notes. You may wish to practice on scrap paper first. Be careful not to smudge the ink! ■

Frosty winter tree

This sophisticated card not only looks good, it's really simple to achieve. The combination of blues and silvers gives a beautiful finish. Anyone receiving this card would truly appreciate it.

YOU WILL NEED

Winter tree stamp 2 x 2 in (5 x 5 cm)
Dye-based ink pads in silver and sky blue
Small piece of white card
Scissors
8¼ x 5¾-in (21 x 15-cm) white card

Scissors
Metal square embossing template
Light box
Low tack masking tape
Embossing tool

Cutting mat
Craft knife
11¾ x 8¼-in (30 x 21-cm) sky blue card
Ruler
3-D foam glue pads

1 Lightly tap the top half of the winter tree stamp with the silver ink pad. Try not to get the ink on the edges of the stamp because this may spoil your stamped image.

2 Next, ink the lower half of the stamp with the sky blue ink pad. Stamp the image on a piece of white card large enough to hold the stamp, taking care not to rock the stamp during the process. Set aside to dry for a few minutes and then cut around the image, leaving a small white border around the edge. **steps 3–6 ▶**

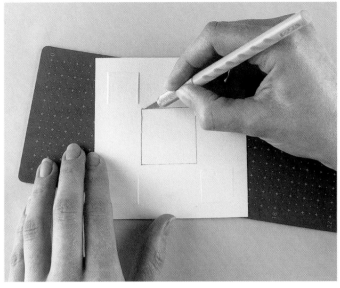

3 Cut a 4½-in (11-cm) square from the 8¼ x 5¾-in (21 x 15-cm) white card. Place the square embossing template on the light box and secure it in place with low tack masking tape. Position the square card on the template and, using the embossing tool, trace out a square at each corner.

4 To create the aperture in the square card, measure a 1½-in (4-cm) square in the center and cut it out over the cutting mat using a craft knife.

5 Cut out a 5½ x 11-in (14 x 28-cm) rectangle from the sky blue card. Score the card down the center lengthwise, using the ruler and the embossing tool, and fold over. Stick 3-D foam glue pads onto the front of the tree design around the white border.

6 Carefully lower the white aperture card from Step 4 over the tree design and, when the design sits straight beneath the aperture, press it firmly down to stick it in place. Place a number of glue pads onto the back of the white card and stick it into place on the front of the sky blue card. ■

Balloons galore

Up, up, and away with these beautiful balloons. Combine punches, stamping, matting, and coloring to create this delightful design. It's great as a party invitation or birthday card for someone with fun in his or her life.

YOU WILL NEED

Balloon punch
8¼ x 5¾-in (21 x 15-cm) purple card
8¼ x 5¾-in (21 x 15-cm) lilac card
8¼ x 5¾-in (21 x 15-cm) pink card
11¾ x 8¼-in (30 x 21-cm) cream
    pearl card

Ruler
Embossing tool
Pencil
Scissors
Craft knife
Cutting mat

Glue stick
Black dye-based ink pad
Balloon stamp 2½ x 1 in (6 x 2.5 cm)
8¼ x 5¾-in (21 x 15-cm) cream card
Pink coloring pencil
3-D gloss

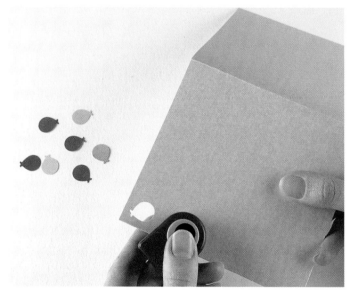

1 Using the balloon punch, punch out several balloon shapes out of the purple, lilac, and pink cards. If you punch the balloons from a strip of paper, the piece that is left over can be used to decorate another card or as a stencil.

2 Cut the 11¾ x 8¼-in (30 x 21-cm) cream pearl card to 5 x 10 in (13 x 26 cm). Score the card down the center lengthwise, using the ruler and the embossing tool, and fold over. Use the balloon punch to punch out a row of balloons along the front right edge of the card. **steps 3–7** ▶

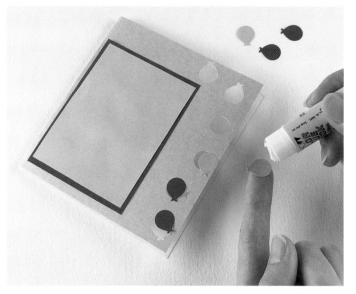

3 Cut out a 3 x 4-in (8 x 10-cm) rectangle from the purple card. Cut out a 2½ x 3½-in (7 x 9-cm) rectangle from the lilac card. Use a pair of scissors or a craft knife over the cutting mat to do this. Glue the purple rectangle onto the front of the cream pearl card, followed by the lilac rectangle over it.

4 Put some glue on part of the back of the purple and lilac balloons and position them so that they partly overlap the punched out balloon shapes on the cream pearl card.

5 Lightly tap the black ink pad onto the balloon stamp and stamp the design onto a piece of cream card large enough to hold the stamp. Take care not to rock the stamp or you may smudge the design. Lift the stamp off cleanly. When dry, cut out around the balloon design so that it is 2 x 2¾ in (5 x 7 cm) in size. Color in the balloon with a pink coloring pencil.

6 Apply 3-D gloss over the pink balloon, holding the bottle sideways over the image, and let the liquid run out on its own. Don't squeeze the bottle or you will get air bubbles. If you do get air bubbles pop them with a pin before the gloss dries. Set aside to dry for a few minutes.

7 Cut a 2¼ x 3-in (6 x 8-cm) rectangle from the pink card. To assemble the card, glue the design centrally over the pink. ■

Enameled heart

Perfect for Valentine's day when you want to tell someone special you care. Try using several colors when embossing to create an enameled look. Torn vellum looks better than regimented straight lines, so experiment tearing scrap pieces of vellum to see how you get on.

YOU WILL NEED

Small piece of white card
Gold pigment-based inkpad
Gold embossing powder
Heat gun
Pencil

Scissors
11¾ x 8¼-in (30 x 21-cm) white card
Ruler
Embossing tool
8¼ x 5¾-in (21 x 15-cm) light gray vellum

8¼ x 5¾-in (21 x 15-cm) white polka dot vellum
8¼ x 5¾-in (21 x 15-cm) pale blue pearl card
Micro glue dots

1 Wipe the gold inkpad over the surface of the small piece of white card. Sprinkle the gold embossing powder over the ink while it is still wet. Tap off the excess powder and return it to the pot. Hold the heat gun 6 in (15 cm) away from the card until the powder has melted. While the powder is still hot, sprinkle on some more powder and tap off the excess. Reapply the heat to melt the second coat and repeat a third time.

2 When the gold enameling has cooled slightly, pencil in a heart shape over it and cut it out using scissors.
steps 3–6 ▶

3 Place the heart onto a spare piece of card with the enameled side uppermost. Hold the heat gun 6 in (15 cm) over the heart and apply the heat to the edges, being careful not to burn your design. Heat the heart until you can see the enamel begin to move.

4 Cut out a 5 x 10-in (12.5 x 25-cm) rectangle from the 11³/₄ x 8¹/₄-in (30 x 21-cm) white card. Score the card down the center lengthwise, using the ruler and the embossing tool, and fold over. To tear the light gray vellum, hold it down firmly with one hand while gently tearing it with the other, as shown. Tear a 3¹/₂-in (7-cm) square.

5 From the white polka dot vellum, tear a 2¹/₂-in (6-cm) square. Cut a 2-in (5-cm) square from the pale blue pearl card. Stick the layers of vellum together rubbing some micro glue dots onto the center of each vellum layer so that they do not show through. Apply some micro glue dots to the back of the pearl pale blue card and stick this onto the center of the vellums. Again using sticky dots, apply some to the center of the pale blue vellum and stick this to the front of the white card.

6 To finish the card, apply micro glue dots to the back of the light gray vellum and fix it on the front of the card. Repeat the process with the polka dot vellum and position it in the middle of the gray vellum. Finally, apply micro glue dots to the back of the enameled heart and position it in the center of the baby blue square. ■

Sunflowers and butterflies

Sunflowers and butterflies are always popular. This is a lovely birthday, get well soon, or just thinking of you card. Brighten someone's day with these merry and cheerful colors.

YOU WILL NEED

11¾ x 8¼-in (30 x 21-cm) cream card
Pencil
Craft knife
Cutting mat
Ruler
Embossing tool

Dye-based ink pads in green and black
Butterfly stamp 1 x 1 in (2.5 x 2.5 cm)
Flower-in-a-vase stamp
  2½ x 1¼ in (6 x 3 cm)
Fiber tip pens in green, orange, and yellow
Scissors

8¼ x 5¾-in (21 x 15-cm) yellow card
8¼ x 5¾-in (21 x 15-cm) green card
Glue stick
3-D gloss
3-D foam glue pads

1 Cut out a 5 x 10-in (13 x 26-cm) rectangle from the 11¾ x 8¼-in (30 x 21-cm) cream card using the craft knife and cutting mat. Score the card down the center lengthwise, using the ruler and the embossing tool, and fold over. Lightly tap the green ink pad over the butterfly stamp, ensuring the surface of the stamp is evenly coated. Stamp the design randomly onto the front of the card, re-inking as necessary and making sure not to rock the stamp during the process because this will smudge the design.

2 On the remaining cream card, stamp the butterfly design again, this time using the black ink pad. Now coat the flower-in-a-vase stamp with the black ink pad and stamp the design onto the remaining cream card. When dry, color in the butterfly and the flower design with green, orange, and yellow fiber tip pens—or your favorite colors. Cut around the butterfly, being extra careful around its delicate antennae. Cut out the flower-in-a-vase design, leaving a small border around it. **steps 3–5 ▶**

3 To assemble the layers, glue the flower design onto a piece of yellow card slightly larger than the card the flower is on. Stick the yellow card onto a piece of green card slightly larger than the yellow card.

4 Apply 3-D gloss over the flower design. Don't squeeze the bottle or you will get air bubbles. If you do get air bubbles pop them with a pin before the gloss dries. Set aside to dry for a few minutes.

5 To assemble the card, stick down the layers at an angle on the front of the cream card. Place a 3-D foam glue pad at the back of the butterfly and position it at the top right-hand corner of the card. ■

A dalliance with dragonflies

The long border stamp has a very stylish feel to it. I have stamped onto blue paper and used colored pencils to color in the image. Torn paper layered under the stamp completes the look for a quick and easy card that takes minutes to make.

YOU WILL NEED

11¾ x 8¼-in (30 x 21-cm) cream card
Ruler
Pencil
Scissors
Embossing tool
Dye-based ink pads in purple and black

Small dragonfly stamp
Dragonflies border stamp
8¼ x 5¾-in (21 x 15-cm) blue paper
Colored pencils in pink,
	purple, and lime green
Paintbrush

8¼ x 5¾-in (21 x 15-cm) purple card
Glue stick
3-D gloss

1 Cut a 8-in (20-cm) square from the 11¾ x 8¼-in (30 x 21-cm) cream card. Score the card down the center lengthwise, using the ruler and the embossing tool, and fold over. Lightly tap the purple ink pad over the small dragonfly stamp and stamp a row of dragonflies down the front right-hand side of the card, re-inking as necessary. Take care not to rock the stamp during the process because this will smudge the design.

2 Lightly tap the black ink pad over the dragonflies border stamp and position it over a strip of blue paper long enough to hold the design, applying even pressure along the length of the stamp. You may want to practice on a piece of scrap paper first. Set aside to dry for a few minutes. **steps 3–6 ▶**

3 Color in the dragonflies using a selection of colored pencils. Trace color around the swirls on the design to create a shadow effect.

4 Place the ruler along the length of the stamped dragonfly image and run a clean wet paintbrush along the edge of the ruler to soften the paper. Carefully tear the paper away. Repeat on all three remaining sides.

5 Cut a rectangle of cream card slightly larger than the torn blue paper. Next, cut a piece of purple card slightly larger than the cream paper. Stick the layers together, with the largest at the bottom, and position onto the front of the stamped cream card.

6 Finally, apply 3-D gloss to the dragonflies, taking care not to squeeze the bottle when applying it because this will create air bubbles. If you do get air bubbles, pop them with a pin before the gloss dries. Set aside to dry for a few minutes. ■

Templates

Fold

Fall leaves
pages 16–17

Fold

Fold

Daisy, daisy
pages 18–19

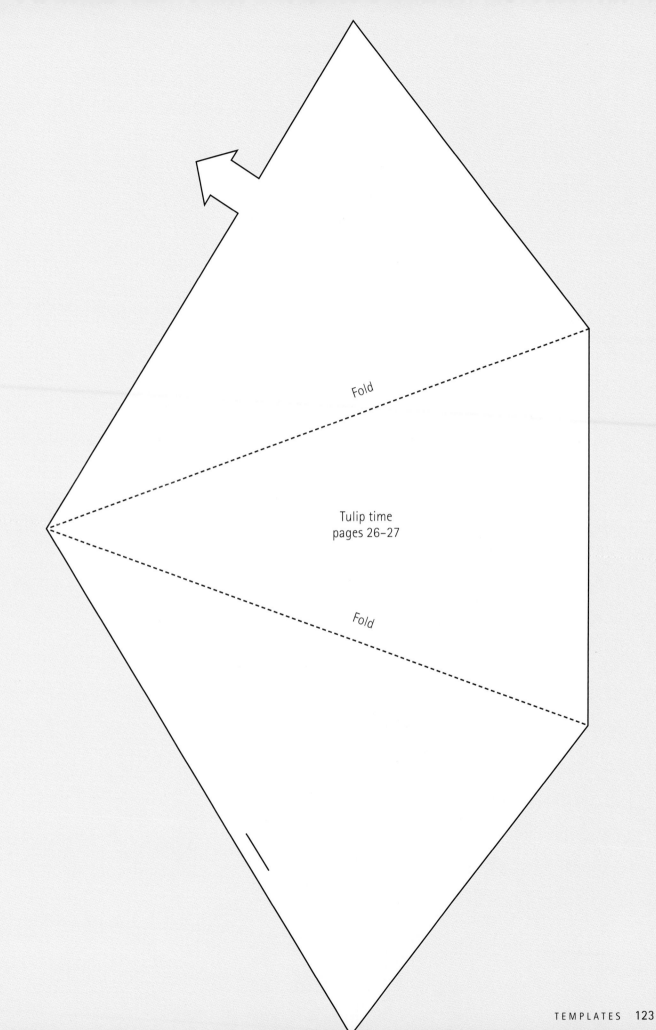

Fold

Tulip time
pages 26–27

Fold

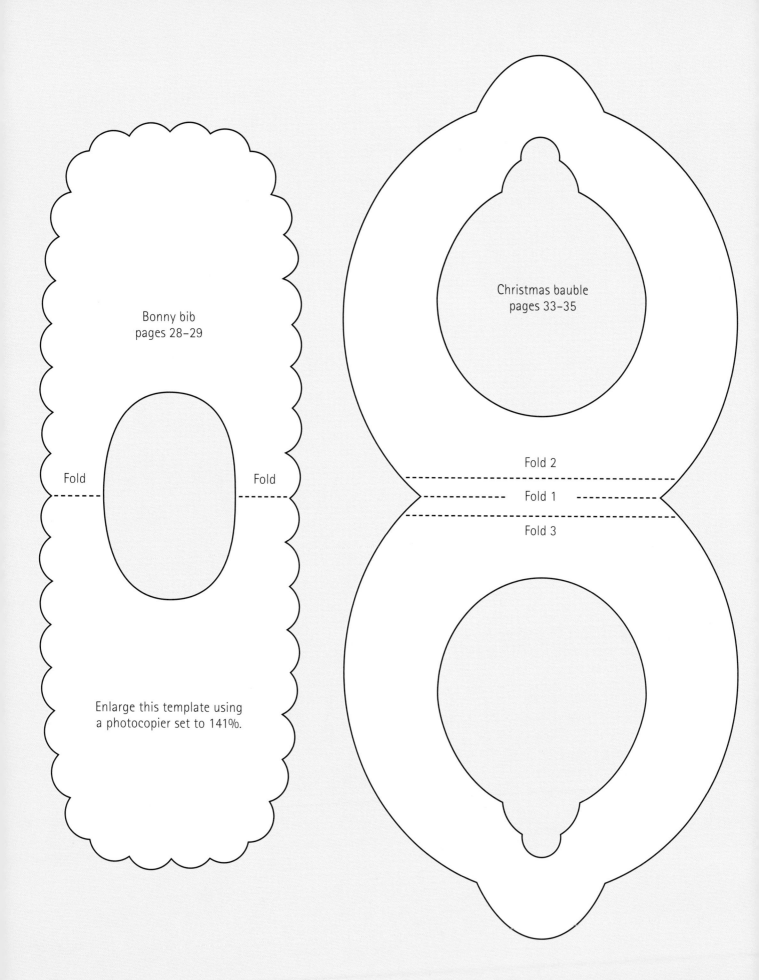

Bonny bib
pages 28–29

Fold

Fold

Enlarge this template using
a photocopier set to 141%.

Christmas bauble
pages 33–35

Fold 2

Fold 1

Fold 3

Spirelli rose
pages 61–63

Embossed
delight
pages 58–60

Birthday purse
pages 81–83

Fold

Fold

Fold

Fold

Fold

Enlarge this template using
a photocopier set to 141%.

Spirelli rose
pages 61–63

Spirelli rose
pages 61–63

Enlarge this group of three
templates using a photocopier
set to 141%.

Iris folding

Musical notes
pages 104–106

Delightful daisy tags
pages 96–98

Suppliers

The following list of companies are suppliers of some of the products used in this book. The page numbers in brackets refer to projects that contain materials available from that particular supplier. Your local craft store will also stock a good range of stencils, stickers, and stamps. Some are suppliers to the trade only. Contact the company or visit the website for a full list of retail stockists.

UNITED STATES

Michaels Arts and Crafts
(general craft supplier)
8000 Bent Branch Drive
Irving, TX 75063
Tel: +1 (214) 4091300
Web: www.michaels.com

Hobby Lobby
(general craft supplier)
7707 SW 44th Street
Oklahoma City, OK 73179
Tel: +1 (405) 7451100
Web: www.hobbylobby.com

Plaid
(trade supplier)
3225 Westech Drive
Norcross, GA 3009-23500
Tel: +1 (678) 2918100
Web: www.plaidonline.com

UNITED KINGDOM

Art and Crafts Direct (pp 18, 42)
(mail order/general craft suppliers)
Unit 44 Coney Green Business Park
Wingfield View
Clay Cross
Derbyshire S45 9JW
Tel: +44 (0)1246 252313
Web: www.artandcraftsdirect.com

Artoz (pp 16, 26, 28)
(stickers and general paper suppliers)
Tannery Court Business Centre
Knight Road
Strood
Rochester
Kent ME2 2JH
Tel: + 44 (0)1634 722060
Web: www.artoz.co.uk

Clarity Stamps
Ludwells Farm
Spode Lane
Cowden
Kent TN8 7HN
Tel: +44 (0)1342 850111
Web: www.claritystamp.co.uk

Design Objectives (p 45)
(trade supplier)
4–8 Fleets Industrial Estate
Willis Way
Poole
Dorset BH15 3SU
Tel: +44 (0)1202 679976
Web: www.docrafts.co.uk

Hobby Craft (pp 36, 39, 45)
(general craft supplier)
Stores throughout the UK
Tel: 0800 027 3387
Web: www.hobbycraft.co.uk

Personal Impressions
(trade suppliers)
Curzon Road
Chilton Industrial Estate
Sudbury
Suffolk CO10 2XW
Tel: +44 (0)1787 375241
Web: www.richstamp.co.uk (for stockists)

Trim Craft (p 30)
Basford Works
Egypt Road
New Basford
Nottingham NG7 7GD
Tel: +44 (0)115 9787899
Web: www.trimcraft.co.uk (for stockists)

Viking Industrial Products Ltd (p 23)
Unit 1 Coronation Business Park
Hard Ings Road
Keighley
West Yorkshire BD21 3ND
Tel: +44 (0)1535 610373
Web: www.vikingtapes.co.uk

HOLLAND/GERMANY/FRANCE

Kars and CO BV (pp 20, 33)
(craft suppliers)
Industrieweg 27
Industriesterrein De Heuning
Postbus 97
4050 EB Ochten
Tel: +31 344642864
Web: www.kars.nl (retail stockists)

SOUTH AFRICA

Art Crafts and Hobbies
72 Hibernia Street
PO Box 9635
George 6530
Tel: +27 (0)44 874 1337

Crafty Supplies
Shop UG 104 The Atrium
Main Road
Claremont
Cape Town
Tel: +27 (0)21 671 0286

L&P Stationery and Artists Requirements
65b Church Street
Bloemfontein
Tel: +27 (0)51 430 1085

AUSTRALIA

Anderson Arts and Crafts
64-68 Violet Street
Revesby
NSW 2212
Tel: +61 (0)20 9772 1066

Edgeworth Craft supplies
63 Edgeworth David Avenue
Waitara
NSW
Tel: +61 (0)20 9489 3909

Craft Warehouse Shop
Campbell Street
Bowen Hills
QLD 4006
Tel: +61 (0)7 3257 1739

Lincraft
Gallery Level
Imperial Arcade
Pitt Street
Sydney
NSW 2000
Tel: +61 (0)20 9221 511

Index